CARRY-*On*
BAGGAGE

Our Nonstop
Flight

Carry-on Baggage *Our Nonstop Flight*

ISBN-10: 0989752615
ISBN-13: 978-0-9897526-1-9

Library of Congress Control Number: 2013946379

Printed in the United States

Published by:

GRIFFIN
SCOTT PRESS
INDIE BESTSELLER PUBLISHING HOUSE

CARRY-*On*
BAGGAGE
Our Nonstop Flight

CYNTHIA BAILEY THOMAS & PETER THOMAS

For my Noelle

I love you,
Mom

For my girls
Porsche Thomas and Blaze Tiangco Thomas

I love you,
Dad

Acknowledgments

First and foremost, we would like to acknowledge God, the driving force in our lives. We are truly just along for the ride; without Him, there would be no us.

We are forever grateful to our families for their encouragement and for giving us an amazing support system to do what we do. You are constant and always there when we are in need. Our journey will always be all about family.

We would like to extend a special thank you to our base of loyal, amazing friends. There are far too many of you to name, but you know who you are. Your friendship means everything to us.

We would also be remiss if we did not thank those who made this project possible:

> Griffin Scott Press, our publisher
> Rochelle Short, our amazing editor
> Derek Blanks, our talented photographer, business partner and friend
> Keith Saunders, our incredible cover designer
> Nataki StarTaki Hair, Cynthia's hairstylist
> Jeremy Dell, Cynthia's makeup artist
> The Bailey Agency School of Fashion
> *The Real Housewives of Atlanta* cast
> Double XXposure Media Relations
> Caliber Enterprises
> True Entertainment
> Bravo

Last but not least, we want to acknowledge our fans for all your unconditional love and continued interest in all we do.

We love you all,
Cynthia & Peter

Contents

CHAPTER I

Prepare for Takeoff
Our Beginning

Peter's Aisle View

P EOPLE ASSUME CYNTHIA and I met a few years before joining our reality show, but our relationship has been a cat-and-mouse
chase spanning twenty years. The first time we met was in 1988 at
Nell's Supper Club. It was the most exclusive club in downtown New York
and a playground for the *Who's Who* of A-list celebrities. You could always
find the house packed with musicians, rappers, actors and models, but no
one ever asked for pictures or autographs. It wasn't a place where enter-
tainers felt like they were the shit, because anything with a pulse inside of
Nell's was hot.

Nell's was actually infamous for turning away the famous, but getting
in the mix wasn't just about being a celebrity. You could've been the cool-
est cat on your block or a star on the rise and still could mingle with
Nell's rich and famous. You had to have the right flava and swag or you
basically spent the night waiting in line. It was an "it" factor that couldn't
be defined in words, people wore it, but the doorman had to believe the
hype too.

Nell's doormen guarded the roped-off, front entrance like the gates of Buckingham Palace. They would walk a line of people that ran almost the entire length of the block, handpicking who went inside. They most definitely had the power to make your night or fuck it up. You were completely at their mercy. Even money couldn't get you through the doors – you could forget about slipping a doorman $500 and sliding inside. Nell's was all about power and status and if you didn't have one (sometimes both), you didn't cross the threshold. It was the Studio 54 of our time, without the drugs – *at least not openly.*

I was the suave, boss-type who fit the bill. For me, getting into Nell's was never an issue. One of the doormen and I were cool because we lived in the same Brooklyn neighborhood. Regardless of having him as a hookup on the door, I had the pull and arrogance to get in just on the strength of my confidence. My vibe was always, *"I'm supposed to get in, and I'm going in."* I knew it, and everybody else did too.

Sundays at Nell's was always crazy poppin' with a massive wait. The night I met Cynthia, Prince was performing, which made it even more of a madhouse. I arrived earlier than usual that evening, hollered at my boy on the door and right as I was about to go in, a second doorman put the brakes on me. I could see he was about to give priority access to a long, shiny, black limousine that pulled up. I was like, *"What the hell? This must be Prince if dude was blocking the door for anybody over me."*

The limo driver got out and opened the back door for a grocery bag of drop-dead, fine girls who strutted out one by one. They were all fly as hell and moved in sync like the cast of Robert Palmer's "Addicted to Love" video. At the time, I didn't realize they were all models. I distinctly remember there being about seven white girls and Cynthia was the lone, black stallion pulling up the rear. Let's be clear though, I noticed her because she was the most striking, not because of the color of her skin. I was feeling her the minute I laid eyes on her. Inside the club, I made it my business to find this chick that stood out from her pack.

I found her seated at a table with her model entourage and offered to buy her a drink. She accepted but asked if I would get a round for her harem of friends too. Being Peter Thomas and feeling myself to the fullest extent, a request to buy drinks for a table of girls never fazed me. Besides, I knew I couldn't get closer to Cynthia without hooking up the rest of her crew.

Realizing she was young and green, I decided not to push up on her. She seemed like an upstate girl, and I knew for sure that she wasn't from the city. Girls from upstate were different from round the way girls – like comparing liver pâté to fried chicken. Not to forget, Nell's was the kind of joint where lions went to get lambs. But on the real, back then Cynthia was too young of a lamb, even for me. She appeared inexperienced and not worth the kill. Basically, she was at an age that would've taken all the thrill out of the victory. So I kept it moving and went home with the bartender that night. She was my supermodel stunt double for the evening. *Damn, what was her name?*

Cynthia's Aisle View

As strange as it sounds, I don't have a clear memory of meeting Peter that first time at Nell's, but his rendition seems familiar. The first encounter I remember was in 1992, on a flight from Miami to New York. I had just wrapped shooting a commercial for Macy's and was on my way back home. I was sitting in first class and recognized Lyor Cohen, an old friend I'd met through my ex-boyfriend, Russell Simmons. Lyor was the former president of Def Jam Records and was traveling with Peter. He introduced us and suggested we get to know each other. Figuring Lyor was up to some mile-high matchmaking, I went with the flow and switched seats with him.

I remember sitting next to Peter, trying to be as cordial as possible, but the whole time I was thinking, *"Wow, what a smart and interesting guy."* We had great, stimulating conversation that flowed effortlessly. I was a

3

little surprised when he didn't ask for my phone number at the end of the flight. I don't remember if I was in a relationship at the time, but getting his number was out of the question for me. That just wasn't my style. Peter was also very vague about his personal information, giving me the impression he had a situation (or two) going on.

From our in-flight conversation, it was apparent we had a lot of mutual friends. In the back of my mind, I anticipated bumping into him at some point in our social circles. Much to my astonishment though, we spent the next fifteen years more like two locomotives steamrolling past each other in the night. Both being industry people, we were always attending the same events and rubbing shoulders with the same people – *but never at the same time*. There was some sort of divine intervention that kept us one step behind the other.

Peter's Boarding Pass

When Lyor introduced me to Cynthia, I felt like I had the upper hand because I had more backstory on her than she had on me. I knew she was the girl who had kicked off record mogul Russell Simmons' model obsession. I didn't know if they were still together, so I didn't try to get her number or make anything pop off.

We shared a lot of the same friends and associates, and my top go-to guys in the industry knew her well. I'd never heard anything bad about her. She stood out to me because she wasn't all extra and over the top. The models I'd met and dated were either really smart or really stupid. Cynthia was in the smart minority. I saw her as a powerful, strong, African American woman who was wrapped tight. SOLID.

The only time she lost points with me was when I heard through the industry grapevine that she was dating this record company executive. He was a dopey, inexperienced kind of dude. Nice, just not a sharp guy who could hold his own, and damn sure not the caliber of guy I thought Cynthia would date. On the other hand, Russell was a crazy, hunter-type;

I knew him to be a visionary and a leader. This record executive cat was like the prey Russell would eat for a light snack. I could never see the correlation between Cynthia and that dude. They just always struck me as an odd combination, like eating caviar on a hotdog bun.

Some people sip from the fountain of destiny – I shower in it. I never doubt that what is meant to be will eventually be. Several years after sitting next to Cynthia on that flight, I met up with our mutual friend, Melrose. In their younger days, she and Cynthia modeled together in New York and Paris. Melrose and I were having lunch and she asked if I remembered Cynthia Bailey. Did I remember her? Of course I did! How could I forget *The Cynthia Bailey*? That beautiful girl from Nell's who I'd shared a plane ride with to New York.

Over the years, I felt like I'd been watching Cynthia from a distance as her career blew up. I would constantly see her face gracing the cover of magazines, catalogs and billboards. I'd also heard that she and Russell were no longer together. Word on the street was that she was a successful woman who only dated brothers that really had it going on. She wasn't out there riding the gravy train, though. By all accounts, Cynthia was an independent woman, doing her thing and signing her own checks.

Melrose was temporarily working for me and knew I was looking for a vehicle. I was two years out of a five-year relationship with the mother of my youngest child. It was a bad breakup, and I wasn't trying to hop into another relationship with anybody. I'd just moved to Atlanta from Miami, and my focus was on handling my business affairs. I was in a new city, meeting new people and starting a new life. Getting my head right and life on track was priority one.

In a weird twist of fate, Melrose told me Cynthia was storing a Range Rover in Atlanta that she didn't need in New York. She mentioned to Cynthia that I was looking for a ride, and Cynthia gave Melrose permission to pass along her number. Who would have known that my car search would be the catalyst for face time with my elusive mystery woman?

I felt like "The Man" that first time I dialed her number and heard her voice on the other end. Somewhere in that initial conversation I asked if she was dating anybody. I knew she had a child with actor Leon Robinson, and I wanted to assess her situation right off the top. The New York social scene was a tight group. If you even casually mentioned a dude's girl by name he was quick to pee and mark his territory in case a predator came sniffing.

I didn't have those boyish, bullshit insecurities because I was always surrounded by gorgeous females. Whether the relationship was romantic or platonic – beautiful women liked being in my world. I was a man accustomed to dining at five-star restaurants and having the finer things at my fingertips. Cynthia was on the level, but I wasn't going in with the fullness until I knew her status.

Her vibe was smooth as hell, and she always made me feel like I could ask her anything. The tone of her voice was so soothing, *borderline hypnotic.* No hype. No urgency. I would ask a question and she would give a straight answer. Even if I was being intrusive, she kept it cool as a grape Kool-Aid. The longer we talked, the more it came back to me how calm and collected she'd been on the plane ride we shared.

I was never one of those guys to do hours of pillow talk on the phone with females, *unless they had something I wanted.* In that case, I would do whatever I needed to do until I got what I was after. With Cynthia, I found myself restless for those late-night talks, and I wasn't shy about initiating calls on the regular. I was drunk with curiosity and wanted to know everything she was willing to tell me about her, and more.

After my first call, we talked on the phone almost daily for six weeks. Melrose would get mad and remind me, "I'm hooking you up to get a damn vehicle, not a date." I never knew why the hell it mattered to her. My dealings with Melrose were only on a business tip and we never had any intimate ties. She had a baby with a popular dude in the recording industry, but they had split up. I was just trying to be a shoulder for her to lean on, help pay her rent, keep the lights on or whatever she needed. It was clear that she liked a brutha and wanted more between us, but I wasn't on that page. I was checking for the supermodel.

Cynthia was scheduled to come to Atlanta on two occasions to finalize my purchase of her truck. She postponed the initial visit because her fortieth birthday had her locked down in Vegas. It felt like she was partying out west for weeks. The more she delayed her trip to Atlanta, the more interested I became. I kept putting my anxiety to see her on needing transportation. Real talk, it was never about buying the Range Rover – *I was falling hard for Cynthia.*

Whenever we spoke, I was relentless in trying to pin her down on a solid date for her visit. I was deflated when she canceled the second time and said it would be another week before she could come. It wasn't an emotion I was used to feeling, especially for a woman I hadn't had sex with. I was feigning to see her so badly that I went to her modeling agency's website to check out her portfolio. I was like, *"Damn, I don't remember her looking this hot!"* I didn't think it was possible. She was so different.

My two previous relationships were with Latin women and the last one left the taste of cyanide in my mouth. The breakup had me completely checked out of the relationship scene. Coming to Atlanta in my mid-forties and dating twenty-something-year-old girls was like spraying Lysol on shitty carpet. I went from bad to worse. After going out with a dozen or so women in that age group, you realize they're basically all alike: same age, same schooling and same amount of brain cells.

Each with a kid (or two, or three, or four), three-bedroom townhouse, nice mid-size car and not a goddamn idea where they want to be in ten years. They're all a fucking headache waiting to happen. Any real dude wouldn't hesitate to admit that his worst nightmare is getting into a relationship with a woman who is about to go through some drama he's already been through. So after a few months of testing the waters in Atlanta, I wasn't hyped about swimming in its dating pool. If I had a change of heart to kick it with someone exclusively, a woman like Cynthia would be my only exception.

Getting to know her was tripping me out. Just a couple of years before we hooked up, I was riding the subway in New York and saw her on a Virginia Slims cigarette poster. Even then, I wondered why this gorgeous-ass woman kept popping up everywhere I went. She was so pretty. The ad had me fantasizing the whole train ride home.

I typically daydreamed on my commute anyway, but that day I couldn't take my eyes off the black beauty plastered on that print ad. It was one of those crazy kind of ads that no matter how I turned or repositioned, her eyes followed me. It freaked me out! Before I got off that train, I had to glance back one last time at those alluring eyes that had stalked me the entire time. I could still see hints of that young lamb from Nell's, who'd shown me no real interest the first night we met. Now, years later, here she was standing in a sultry pose, smoking a cigarette and staring me down. All I could think was, *"Oh! Okay, now honey wanna sweat me."*

Cynthia's Boarding Pass

I guess the third time must really be the charm – or at least it was with me and Peter. I'd been working in New York since graduating from high school in 1985. I was busting my ass and making a crap load of money, so in 2006 I decided to treat myself to a new Range Rover. It didn't take long for me to realize you don't need a Range Rover in New York City. I eventually found someone in Atlanta to take over the payments in a sublease, but the leasee defaulted on the payments. Until I could figure out a plan for the truck, I had my cousin (who lived in Atlanta) store it in his garage.

The following year, I reconnected with my friend Melrose, who'd recently moved to Atlanta from Miami. She was working as Peter's administrative assistant while he was building his new restaurant, Uptown. I considered it a blessing in disguise when she told me he was looking for a truck. I remembered Peter from the plane ride in '92, and over the years his name had come up several times in industry conversations. From dating Russell and hearing him talk about Peter, I knew Peter was a man that he respected. One year, Russell even served as a keynote speaker at Peter's "How Can I Be Down?" music convention.

I told Melrose she could pass along my phone number to Peter if he wanted to call and make arrangements to see the truck. I still smirk remembering the first time he called pretending to only be interested in the vehicle. He asked all kinds of inappropriate questions that made it clear to me he was looking for more than just a ride. "How's your career going? How old are you? What agency are you with? How long have you been in New York?"

His questions had absolutely nothing to do with buying my truck. I thought, *"This man is either truly curious about my life or really interested in me."* But I liked the tone of his voice and felt some kind of connection in that first call. He spiked my curiosity, similar to how a person's smile or walk can grab your attention at a glance. He also initiated a lot of small talk, but seemed comfortable being direct. His approach was very assured, very bold and very confident. I found it all rather obnoxious, but I was inexplicably enticed by his style.

Despite his allure, there were some contradictions in his personality that occasionally threw me. Like the time I had to take an incoming call during one of our conversations and told him I'd call him back. When I did, a female answered his phone and said, "Peter's eating right now." Really? This man who'd called me daily and asked me every personal question short of when I had my last period was now playing me like he was King Henry VIII? All of a sudden he was too occupied to bring his black ass to the phone? Wow!

I was accustomed to a man sprinting to the phone when I called. I was surprised when Peter didn't drop what he was doing to talk to me. It wasn't the reaction I was used to receiving from the opposite sex. Despite those contrasts in his disposition, I was always giddy when his number popped up on my call display. But I refused to read too much into my feelings. I knew no matter how much we connected by phone, I still needed to assess my level of interest face-to-face. At best, I was intrigued and excited to see what he'd be like in person.

The day we finally met turned out to be a *close encounter of the strangest kind*. Melrose was supposed to pick me up from the airport but got stuck at work. Instead, she sent Peter to the rescue. The bigger issue was that I'm a girl who's big on comfort, and I never *fly pretty*. When I realized Peter was filling in for Melrose, I texted him and lied that my flight had been delayed. I needed to stall him long enough to get my cute on. My backstage runway skills came in handy that day, and I evoked my sixty-second-transformation superpower.

I had this unnerving feeling in my stomach that I use to get when I was younger; some people refer to it as butterflies. I felt so silly and high school. I couldn't figure out why I was so nervous and fidgety to see Peter. Why did I want to make such a lasting impression on a man I didn't really know? I wondered if my feelings were all over the place because it was such a weird situation or because I was starting to like him. I tried my best to remove all expectations from my head, but my brain was on autopilot.

Everything felt so new and peculiar. There were definitely reactions going off in my body that I hadn't experienced before. The element of the unknown was starting to tempt me. I was going to Atlanta for two days, this guy was picking me up and the experience would either be really triumphant or really tragic. As crazy as it sounds, I felt like I was going to be on the next flight home or never going back at all. I just knew something life-altering would happen that weekend.

I was standing outside at baggage claim when I saw my truck pull up. Newsflash: it was *not* love at first sight for me. Peter looked different (juicier and rounder) than I recalled from our plane encounter. Sitting next to him, he looked like a bigger, more mature version of himself. I wasn't physically attracted and remember thinking it would definitely be one of those weekends where beauty would be in the eye of the *beer-holder*.

He asked if I needed to be anywhere or minded rolling with him to run some errands. Again, here comes the crazy. I didn't really know this man and shouldn't have even been alone with him in the vehicle. Yet, there I was, about to run errands with this stranger behind the sexy phone voice.

He asked with such a sense of normalcy that I felt comfortable going along for the ride. I figured at least one of us had to be out of our minds or *on something,* because it just wasn't usual behavior.

Not even five minutes after agreeing to ride along, Peter's Alex Trebek hat was on and in full effect. He was firing off questions as if I was a *Jeopardy!* game show contestant. "Why aren't you married? What kinds of houses do you like? How much longer do you plan on modeling? Do you want more kids? What happened in your last relationship?" It was as if I'd stepped off the plane and right into the twilight zone. His questions were over the top and as prying as they were, I answered every damn one. My heart told me they weren't the kind of questions a man asked if he was just trying to hit it. I knew I was talking to a grown man who had been through some shit.

Everything shifted for me as we talked during the ride. I became more attracted and involved in getting to know him. He continued his rapid-fire ambush of questions. "How do you like the brick color on the front of that house? How do you feel about the master bedroom being on the main level?" This man took intrusive to a whole new level, but strangely, I was enjoying our conversation. *If I can even call it that!*

It was very much an out-of-body experience for me. I was starting to lose control over my responses to this alpha man. I found myself over-answering questions and being super chatty – something I only do when I'm out of my comfort zone. Truthfully, every minute I spent with Peter left me itching to learn all I could about him. It was time for me to activate my A-game.

From that point on, I knew I needed to sound good, smell good and look good. How in the hell was I going to do it all, without A-game fragrance, gear or shoes? Originally, my plan was just to dip into Atlanta, close the deal on the truck and head back to New York. I was staying at the home of Boris Kodjoe and Nicole Ari Parker Kodjoe.

Boris and I modeled together and had been friends for over twenty years. After they married, Nicole and I had also grown close. They would always invite me to visit them in Atlanta, but the weekend I finally decided to come, they were out of town. With them gone, I had planned to just rough it for the weekend and kick back at their place – minus the glam factor. But the matter had officially been upgraded to a state of emergency.

Peter's Boarding Pass (Part II)

I circled around the damn airport three times waiting for that woman to come out. On the last round, I saw this beautiful, gazelle-like specimen stick her long arm out in front of oncoming traffic. Her head was wrapped in a scarf and she was wearing a gray shawl. She was a straight up, USDA-certified woman. I parked at the curbside long enough to put her bags in, ask how her flight was and begin some small talk. I didn't care what she said; I just wanted to hear her talk. I was reminded of that intoxicating phone vixen and affixed on every word coming from the sexiest lips I'd ever seen. Knowing Cynthia now, her sugary tone is one of the tricks she uses to reel in bruthas and mess with their heads. That shit is like a spider's web.

Before she arrived in Atlanta, she mentioned she'd be staying at Boris and Nicole's house. I'd crossed paths with Nicole in New York and was amped to remind her that we'd met. I was also looking forward to meeting Boris for the first time. It was disappointing to learn from Cynthia that they were out of town and had only offered their place for the weekend. Since I was just dropping her off, I asked if she would ride with me to take care of some business. When she agreed I thought, *"This is going to be easier than I thought."*

Our first stop was to meet one of my boys. Fortunately for me, he was the type of guy who would swear he was ten minutes away, but would really be on the other fucking side of town. I figured I would use the time wisely to put Cynthia through *The Peter Thomas Inquisition*.

I didn't have time for no bullshit. I was focused on asking questions to determine where she stood. Did her daughter live with her? How much longer was she planning to model? I needed to figure out if this woman knew her next move. Her responses would determine if she was someone I wanted to move forward with. It would be hard for her to mess up, because I was more than interested at that point. She was insanely hot. I kept thinking, "*Even if she gives me a whack answer, I may try to make this shit work anyway.*"

She wasn't resisting my inquest and by allowing me to grill her, I knew that she was interested. I was floored when it hit me how beautiful of a woman she was, not only on the outside – but where it counted the most for me – on the inside.

Cynthia was a New York girl, who could have shut my shit down in a heartbeat. Being a New York guy, I would've taken the brick and kept it moving. Sitting in the parking lot that day (waiting for my lying-ass friend), I came to the conclusion that I wanted to give *it* my all. Whatever we were about to do, however it was gonna pop off, I was prepared to give 100 percent. It was Friday evening, she was leaving Sunday afternoon and I had forty-eight hours to close both deals (the vehicle *and her*).

CHAPTER II

Companion Pass
Our First Date

Cynthia's Buddy Pass

ON A SCALE of one to five (with five being the pinnacle), after meeting Peter my interest was at a two, *but my curiosity was a four and rising.* His magnetism was the only reasonable explanation for why I'd allowed a virtual stranger to pick me up in a truck that he'd not even purchased. Even weirder, I was sitting next to him in a part of town I knew nothing about and still under the veil of his interrogation. If his strip mall probe was our unofficial first date, it had to be the least charming I'd ever experienced. *I'd had more romantic pap smears.*

We spent most of the time talking about me, with him being careful not to reveal too much about himself. He was skilled at saying a lot while telling nothing. He had this uncanny ability to be direct and vague at the same time. I sensed there was more to him than he was sharing. I'm also woman enough to admit my actions were a true indicator of how much I'd started to let my guard down. At that point in my day, I'd planned to be sitting somewhere in a swank bar having cocktails with Melrose. Yet there I was, still with Peter, *in a Kroger parking lot.*

Several hours after being kidnapped and surviving my unsolicited tour of Atlanta, we finally reached Boris and Nicole's house. As I got out of the car, Peter reminded me he'd return later to pick me up for the dinner party he was throwing for Melrose's birthday.

Getting dressed for dinner, our day together kept replaying in my head like a scratched record. My reflecting created more contradictions than clarity. Over the years, I'd gotten both favorable and less-than-desirable feedback about Peter. Some of it left me with an impression that he was a made-guy from the streets who'd come checking on a John Gotti tip if he had a problem with somebody. I'd heard he was a hard worker and a hustler who took the music industry under his wings. He wasn't one of those guys from the suburbs that the industry sucked in as an intern, pushed up the corporate ladder and manufactured into a cookie-cutter executive.

Peter had street cred. Even though other industry guys I'd dated were bosses, they were behind-the-desk guys. Men who lived in a fantasy world, selling music about things they knew little about. *Making songs about hustlin' ain't the same as being a hustler.* From dating Russell, I knew Peter was legendary in the industry and a man no one wanted to piss off. Peter was respected by business moguls for not taking shit. His rep was that if he had beef with someone, he'd go see them – and if it got physical – *it got physical.* The guy I'd unexpectedly spent the day with was very different from my grapevine impression. I was becoming more and more enthralled with the man behind the myths.

By the time Peter picked me up later that night for dinner, I'd been in Atlanta for eight hours and he was the only person I'd seen. He looked better than our initial meeting at the airport and cleaned up well – wearing Levi jeans, a crisp white dress shirt and nice leather shoes. Everything looked brand spanking new, like he'd made a mall run before picking me up. The shirt and jeans were on trend, but both were starched stiff enough to stand up on their own and strike a mannequin pose on a dime. *Real old school.*

In New York, starch and creased jeans were serious crimes of fashion. The slim-cut, skinny jean was on the rise, and the oversized look was being laid to rest. Peter's jeans needed to be dropped at least two sizes, the creases belonged on a military uniform and the starch had to go altogether. He reminded me of an old guy trying to rock a younger look, but all the dots didn't connect.

I gave him major props for smelling really good. Well, maybe he was wearing a teeny bit too much cologne, like he should have sprayed two pumps instead of four. Fashion was my thing, and in my opinion all his faux pas were easy fixes. He wasn't even my man, yet there I was, already making him over in my head. Hell, technically we still hadn't been on a first date.

The ride to the restaurant was pleasant, not excessively chatty like before. We had real conversation and much-needed moments of silence for me to process the occurrences of the day. Melrose called to say she was working late again and running behind for her own birthday dinner. The rest of our party was also late, so we perched on a pair of seats at the bar to await everyone's arrival. Our anticipated group of twelve was starting to feel more like an intimate party of two. Every part of the day that was supposed to involve others, kept reducing to just the two of us.

We were both really relaxed after a few cocktails, and Peter was getting finer and finer by the minute. We knocked back about four rounds without food, and it didn't take long for the alcohol to kick in. We weren't drunk but we were feeling real nice. The room was spinning *in a welcoming way.* When Melrose and the other guests arrived two hours later, we were having such an enjoyable time that neither of us had missed them. Their presence gave me that "*damn…damn…damn*" kind of feeling that teenagers get when the chaperones turn up the bright lights on a slow song at the homecoming dance.

It was awkward finally seeing Melrose after almost eight years of estrangement. Outside of her call a few months prior, we hadn't spoken or seen each other since our unjustified fallout. According to her, she'd gone through some recent things that prompted her to reach out and clear the air between us. Before our hiatus, we'd been great friends and I felt the break in communication was over silly, childish insecurities. *Hers, not mine.*

She was the first friend I'd made in New York City. When our careers were climbing at the same pace, things were fine, but I felt a shift in our closeness when my success began to inch past hers. After starting our careers on an equal playing field, witnessing my rise seemed difficult for her. Funny how things turn out, because I never felt I had greater odds of making it. I wasn't skinnier. I wasn't much taller. I wasn't more connected or prettier. We were equals with the same shot at making it big.

We always envisioned ourselves being top models together, jet-setting around the world inseparably. *Unfortunately, it didn't work out that way.* She responded to my success by placing distance between us. She went out of her way to make new friends, and I was compelled to do the same. Not a lot of words were exchanged. It was just one of those salty situations where we both knew what went down but neither ever spoke of it.

Seeing her after so many years, she was still as beautiful as I remembered. We hugged and exchanged pleasantries, "Oh my God, you look great! You grew your hair out!" Blah. Blah. Blah. She seemed eager to pick up where things had left off. We spent the whole night playing catch-up, and Peter seemed perfectly content being excluded from the conversation. He just sat there taking it all in, probably plotting his next move on me.

I sensed Melrose was surprised to see that Peter and I had become rather chummy. Their exchange during dinner seemed friendly, but the more interest I showed in Peter, the more I felt her plans for him exceeded friendship. I got the vibe that my presence was infringing on her Plan B. Peter swore nothing was going on between them, but girl-friend's body language was screaming that she wasn't happy with the obvious attraction brewing between him and me. I didn't necessarily notice any sexual energy between them. However, it was pretty apparent that Melrose wanted to keep her options open with Peter. I smelled sour grapes and wine wasn't on our table.

Peter's Buddy Pass

On a scale of one to five, my interest in Cynthia was a ten and my curiosity was at fifteen. I was a serial dater, but I liked being committed because it kept me grounded and focused on my business. Single life had the opposite effect and tempted my idle mind to wander. I'd always been picky where women were concerned, but just the thought of being in a relationship with Cynthia symbolized stability for me. I'm admittedly a difficult guy who can find ten different reasons in ten seconds not to like a woman. Even if I didn't, most found a way to annoy the hell out of me in the first five minutes of conversation. Not Cynthia. She passed all my preliminary tests with flying colors.

I liked how generous she was in our conversation – answering question after question while we sat in that parking lot. Her face would downright light up every time her daughter Noelle's name came up. I even managed to sneak in a few indiscreet questions about her daughter's father. The sale of her vehicle was the springboard that brought her to Atlanta and back into my life. I had no doubts about the truck; my hesitation was if *she* was a deal worth closing. I didn't know much about modeling, except it eventually slowed down with age. I couldn't imagine why it would for her because she was more radiant than the first time we'd met in her twenties. Until I was able to determine her willingness to be in a committed relationship, I couldn't even see the possibility of her being my woman. I needed to find out everything I could about her.

My questioning started to chip away at her ice block exterior – it didn't last long, though. Our conversation was cut short when my always-running-a-few-minutes-behind, late-ass friend arrived. I'd hoped he'd never show, but now there was no more stalling. Hours had passed since I picked Cynthia up from the airport; the gig was up and it was time to drop her off. I wasn't familiar with the part of town where Boris and Nicole lived so we got lost along the way. When we finally arrived, my high moment with Cynthia hit a brick wall. I remember looking at the outside of their home and feeling like it was a place that signified where I had been and desperately wanted to get back to.

I was sleeping in the guest room of my parents' place – a spot I'd not been since graduating from high school. Just two years before moving in with my folks, I'd worked hard with my ex to build our dream home and walked away from it when we separated. It was just as beautiful as the house that was in front of me. That picturesque mansion with perfect landscaping slapped me in the face with the reality of how much work I needed to do to reclaim my Peter Thomas swagger. Walking Cynthia to the front door was like a rite of passage. I felt more focused than ever on elevating my hustle.

It was four hours roundtrip to drop Cynthia off, drive to my parents' place, change clothes and get back to pick her up. She had no idea the distance I was driving or the hoops I was jumping through to be at her disposal that weekend. Getting ready for Melrose's dinner, I'd grown jittery and stupid tense. I was never uneasy around any woman, but I felt an interest and compatibility with Cynthia that was even greater than what I'd felt for my ex. She was Latina and we didn't speak the same language (figuratively or literally). She and her family could've been in the same room ripping me a new asshole, and I would've thought they were singing me "Happy Birthday."

I was an international lover who dated beautiful women, regardless of their race. Cynthia and I had nice parallels – with her being African American and me being of West Indian descent. She knew what I was saying, and I knew what the fuck she was saying. I loved that we were of the same pigment, age and background. She had the goods to make me want to get my life in order with the quickness. I was forty-six years old, living back at home and in that moment – wiping down buckets of nervous sweat – but on the inside I felt brand new. *I was headed to take Cynthia Bailey to dinner.*

She looked incredible when I returned to pick her up. I can't recall what she was wearing because I couldn't really focus on anything outside of her face. I was trying to find faults, but there were none. At the restaurant, we found two cozy seats at the bar to wait for the rest of our party. The continuance of my interrogation was disturbed by two ladies seated nearby who kept staring and pointing. One finally approached us and asked my stunning date if she was Cynthia Bailey, the model. Cynthia humbly confirmed her suspicion. "I thought you were! My friends and I were just admiring how beautiful you are," the lady shrilled with a sort of tripped-out stare at Cynthia.

The woman was JaQuitta Williams, an Atlanta news anchor. I was blown away by her exchange with Cynthia. How the fuck did this local newswoman recognize a New York-based supermodel? Cynthia really was some kind of celebrity! JaQuitta gestured for her friends to come over, who also greeted Cynthia and asked for pictures. Guess who was the damn photographer for their impromptu photo shoot? It was cool, though. I understood they were admiring her, just as I was.

Melrose's eventual arrival at dinner was a non-factor. She'd picked up on how much I liked Cynthia and started feeling me for all the wrong reasons. She was unhappy in a deteriorating relationship and constantly needed my ear. I limited my role to that of a big brother. She was like the little sister who always managed to put herself in a predicament that called for me to bail her out. Even though she was an attractive woman, I didn't feel anything sexual toward her. We'd never kissed or dated, and only went out on a strictly platonic tip. One of our wee-morning outings had even ended with her staying overnight in a guestroom at my parents' house. There were countless times something physical could have jumped off, but I wouldn't allow it.

It was amusing to see how Cynthia brought out Melrose's competitive edge. She arrived at her birthday dinner looking extra fancy. Granted she was a real pretty girl, but that night she knew she'd be in the company of a thoroughbred, and it was clear she came to run in the same race. As our party was being seated for dinner, we walked directly past a girl I'd slept with a few months back. She was a young tenderoni who really liked me. I admired her ambition, but we were too far apart in age for anything serious to jump off. I was praying the hostess wouldn't seat us at the available table beside her. The hostess obviously sucked at mindreading, because she did the exact damn opposite of what I was thinking and sat us right on the bull's-eye.

I looked over and noticed honey was giving me a couple of real deep cuts with her eyes. They were sharp, slicing wounds. If looks could really cut, I would've needed two blood transfusions that night. Melrose knew the deal between me and the girl and enjoyed the hell out of her silent ambush. Knowing Melrose, she probably wanted the shit to end in a train wreck. *It wasn't happening!*

Number one, I was still a man who knew how to handle his business. Number two, my single focus for the evening was on one woman. Cynthia. Bailey. There could've been a head-on collision coming my way and I wouldn't have noticed. Even before Cynthia's visit to Atlanta, I'd started the process of shutting females down and ripping names from my Little Black Book. Homegirl seated next to us was on one of those torn pages. There was only one course of action to keep the night flowing. I cut and pasted Razor Eyes from the dining room, ordered a couple bottles of wine and a big, juicy steak. End scene.

Cynthia's Voluntary Layover

Following Melrose's birthday dinner and some serious cocktails, I made it back to Boris and Nicole's around one in the morning. And before noon that day, I was sitting back in my truck's passenger seat next to Peter. It was Saturday and he'd volunteered to chauffeur me to Melrose's place since she lived nearly an hour away. Peter was so hyped to show off Atlanta and be my personal tour guide for the day. He still did most of the talking, while my mind wandered and second-guessed my actions over the past twenty-four hours. What the hell was I really doing?

I was mad at myself for getting too tipsy the night before. I should've at least had appetizers before drinking, especially after such a long afternoon of sightseeing with Peter (*if that's what you want to call it*). I tried to discern what I was feeling and why I had so many emotions flowing through me. It felt like I'd taken over someone else's body – or life for that matter. From the time I'd landed in Atlanta the day before, my every action had been totally uncharacteristic.

I also knew I needed to process the weird energy I'd picked up from Melrose at her birthday dinner. I couldn't quite figure out if she was feeling Peter, but I knew for sure she wasn't checking for him to be checking for me. To be completely 100, I felt caught in the middle of some strange chemistry between the two of them. I forced my brain to focus on the task at hand and not go in too deep on whatever side thang they had going on. Bottom line, I was in Atlanta to sell my truck, not peddle drama.

Melrose and her young daughter were living with her sister outside of Atlanta. Her life was far from the stellar days of New York and Paris. She seemed to be starting over from go, and I felt like she was looking for Peter to be her knight in shining armor. At best, *the one* who would rescue her from life's circumstances.

Knowing him like I do now, I can attest to how Peter instinctively goes into relationships (whether romantic or platonic) with a built-in mindset of enhancing them. He's a man's-man who naturally wants to improve situations. It gives him a high knowing he's aided in turning around someone's life. He's the Dalai Lama of analyzing things that are broken and knowing how to elevate them to the next level. Peter was accustomed to being the architect who mapped the path that pushed the women in his life toward greatness. In some of his most significant relationships, he spearheaded his counterpart's success. I could easily see those standout qualities being Peter's Achilles' heel in his friendship with a woman like Melrose.

It made me sad to see Melrose's life idling in the same place. Starting out, we had the same opportunities, but a different drive and hustle. I could have married any millionaire and had instant financial security, but I took pride in working my ass off for every luxury in my life. I wasn't a star or necessarily a household name, but my shit was together. I had no complaints about my life.

I lived in a spacious apartment on the Upper East Side, my daughter was in a great school and I had access to just about any available bachelor. One thing was for sure, I certainly didn't need a prince to sweep me off my feet with a pair of glass slippers and the promise of a fairy-tale ending. Anyone who came into my life could only enrich what was already near-perfect in my eyes. I was completely happy, with sound peace of mind and was by all measures, successful.

Since Melrose lived quite a distance out, Peter hung around while I visited with her for a few hours. Witnessing her new life in Atlanta was tough for me, but the last thing I wanted to do was make her uncomfortable. There were no conversations about going shopping at Louis Vuitton or having a fancy dinner at The St. Regis. I played myself down to the point where I almost felt like I was acting. In no way did I get off on seeing how things had turned for Melrose. It truly made me sad to see how she'd landed.

On the drive back, I was pretty silent and didn't find it appropriate to discuss Melrose or ask Peter what was going on with her. Though I was taken aback by her living situation, it all appeared normal to Peter and Melrose. I didn't read anything from either that conveyed they viewed her living situation as abnormal. If they didn't have a problem with her state of affairs, why the hell would I?

Peter dropped me back at the Kodjoes' house so I could prepare for another night of dinner with him. I'd told him my favorite food on the planet was Japanese, so he offered to take me to Geisha House. Geisha was known for its talented international chefs, fantastic selection of Japanese food and delicious sushi. I was secretly thrilled to spend another evening in Peter's company. He rushed home to shower and change for dinner, and when he returned to pick me up it was like no time had passed. I was getting accustomed to being his wing-woman in the passenger seat. With each tour of the town, my anticipation to be with him grew stronger.

At Geisha, we again met up with Melrose and another group of friends. I noticed Peter was acting differently – edgy and out of sorts. He was walking really fast like a crackhead and stayed in front of me instead of beside me. I could tell he was in his head and something had him distracted. When we were seated, I sat on one side of Peter and Melrose flanked the other. My heart was very much softened by my visit to Melrose's home, and I did my best to be aware of her presence and give her most of my attention. She seemed to be having a good time and her energy was more balanced than the night before.

Aside from Peter's weird streak, dinner at Geisha felt like our real first date. There was a moment in the evening when he laid his hand on my lap. It felt good, and I returned the gesture by placing my hand over his.

It was so hard for me to accept that I liked this guy. I wasn't prepared to fall for him like that. I was a control freak who typically hated surprises. Being in such a situation with a man I'd spent less than twenty-four hours with, infringed on my sense of control. Shit, the act of even placing my hand on his could have been mistaken as a green light for him to move in for the kill.

Once he'd touched me, I noticed a surge in Peter's confidence and his fretfulness completely disappeared. He seemed less awkward and more at ease. He was definitely interested in me, and it was all I needed to know. In my mind, all questions were resolved about him...*and about him and Melrose.* I decided to let go and take a chance on what the weekend would bring.

After dinner, Peter decided our next move would be to his friend's nightclub. It was the first time in a while that I'd partied outside of New York. Atlanta was entertaining and filled with warm people, but it was no New York! It wasn't as exclusive. Wristbands and hand stamps seemed to be a central nightlife theme, making it feel more like a venture to Six Flags. Living in New York created a standard where you go through the world comparing everything to it. I'd experienced the best of everything in New York: best Japanese food, best shopping and the best clubs. It seemed everything I'd ever tried always placed second best to New York. Peter was becoming an obvious exception.

Peter must've felt like a pimp that whole night. Melrose and I had sat on either side of him at dinner, and he'd entered the club with Melrose in one hand and me in the other. We accessed the club through a rear, VIP entrance where Cee Lo Green was standing. I could have sworn he did a double take as I walked past, but I never big-dealed a man's overt attention toward me, especially when I was dressed to slay.

Inside, the night was fueled with drinking, dancing and grown-folks fun. The group of friends who'd met us for dinner at Geisha also joined us at the club. Peter was in alpha-male form buying shots for everyone. The club was packed wall-to-wall, and I needed a break from the crowded dance floor. I was sitting in an upstairs window ledge, one of the only available seats in the house, when Peter walked up and started dancing beside me. He was like a watchdog marking his terrain in a crowded field of pit bulls. I sat there amused, taking in his every antic.

When he knelt down in front of me, I leaned forward, assuming he was trying to speak over the loud music. My lean was intercepted by a gentle, wet peck on the lips. I was shocked by his boldness, but I went with the flow since I didn't detect any halitosis. The kiss was not too aggressive and just enough.

I appreciated a man who was skilled at taking his time. The one-small-step-a-day approach turned me on. I knew Peter wanted to jump in and tear me apart like a rabid dog, which drew me into him even more. I looked to see if anyone, particularly Melrose, observed our kiss. Everyone in our clique appeared to be on their own agenda, showing no interest in either of us. I found it sexy knowing we'd kissed in a crowded room of people and not a soul noticed. Secrets always made things more stimulating for me.

Well into the early hours of Sunday morning, we started our descent back to Boris' house. I was very tipsy *again*. On the ride, I kicked off my shoes, reclined the seat and elevated my legs on the dashboard. Though comfort played a part in my decision to rest my legs on the dash, it was also a little test of Peter's strength. I was wearing a short skirt and when I put my legs up I was borderline exposed. My panties covered the goodies, though.

I was exhausted and slept the entire ride. He allowed me to rest and didn't wake me until we reached the house. I put my shoes on, pulled my skirt down and headed straight for the front door. I didn't even pause to give him a goodnight smack on the lips. I was proud of him for not taking my bait to go fishing.

First thing Sunday morning, my cell phone rang. It was Peter, of course. Eyeballing the alarm, I saw that it was just after eight o'clock. He had to be kidding! I was hung over and still very sleepy. He said he'd made brunch reservations for us at The Ritz-Carlton and was calling to see what time he could scoop me up. Two hours later I was dressed, packed for the airport and waiting to hear Peter pull into the driveway. I must have not been as sleepy as I thought.

At the Ritz, the maître d' addressed us as Mr. and Mrs. Thomas. That normally would've freaked me out, but I thought, *"Okay, I can be Mrs. Thomas for this one brunch."* After all, nothing else that whole weekend had been normal or my typical behavior, so why start adding rules to the playbook in the last quarter? As with every conversation between us that weekend, our talk at brunch peeled back more layers. We had mad chemistry, and I was sure we were at the beginning of something. I still knew barely anything about him, but I very much liked what I was finding out about the sensual Jamaican man.

I'd secretly hoped Peter would take the longest way possible to the airport, but part of me was also anxious to get there, play back and process my last two days in Atlanta. I was tripping like crazy and asking myself a trillion schoolgirl questions in my head. Was he going to kiss me when I got out? What would he think about me after dropping me off? As he pulled into the airport, he asked that I call him once I got through security. I liked his authority and initiative, and I was more than happy to honor his request.

I gathered my things and hurried inside. No kiss this time either, just a lingering hug. Walking away, I figured his eyes would be on my butt, so I hit him with an extra sexy runway walk. It was five seconds of my life that Naomi Campbell didn't have nothing on me. I'd made the trip to Atlanta with the intent of selling my Range Rover, but we never mentioned the purchase once. Yes, it was official. I had lost my damn mind.

Peter's Voluntary Layover

Operating on only a few hours of sleep, I felt like I could run a marathon when I took Cynthia to Melrose's that Saturday morning. Maximizing every minute with her was my primary focus, so I always managed to create detours on our drives. That morning, I took her through one of Atlanta's most beautiful and affluent neighborhoods. We had great conversation about our ambitions, and the drive was another opportunity for me to inquire about how rooted she was in the North. I asked if she would ever leave New York. She said she wouldn't be opposed to the idea, depending on the right circumstances. Twenty-four hours was all the time I had left with her. How could I lock her down before Sunday? My thoughts were all over the place.

I'd been working like a maniac since moving to Georgia, and I had enough cash flow put back to visit Cynthia in New York as often as I wanted. My dad had placed a second mortgage on his home and cosigned for major credit lines totaling about $200K to support my business ventures. He was a loyal, silent partner who always put his money where his mouth was, but trusted me to make all the decisions. I was sitting on another $120K in the bank and preparing to move into a downtown condo that I'd just signed a lease on. I was rubbing shoulders with the right people and had started the process of reinventing myself in Atlanta. My hope was that the woman beside me would want to ride out with a brutha.

At Melrose's place, I tried to give her and Cynthia space to reconnect. I waited around since it would've been a two-hour drive to go home and come back. Plus, I wanted to spend every second possible with Cynthia, even if I was just watching her from afar. The visit was brief and the interaction between the two of them seemed forced. Their drama wasn't my business, though, and I wasn't about to stick my nose in it.

On the drive from Melrose's, Cynthia told me her favorite food in the whole world was Japanese and that she could eat it every day. I figured

I could monopolize more of her time by offering to take her to Geisha House for dinner. After dropping her off, I was back in the routine of racing home to shower, changing clothes and returning to chauffeur her. The distance and turnaround was a pain in the ass, but she was worth every mile I clocked. I was getting excited, realizing she was everything I'd imagined in a wife and soul mate.

She looked unbelievably edible when I returned to get her later that night. I made sure she sat right next to me at the restaurant, *with Melrose's ass on the other side*. Cynthia had extended her the invitation to join us earlier that day. Why was this girl all up under me? If anything, I thought she would've rather sat next to Cynthia to continue their girl talk. Instead, I was sandwiched between the two, and Melrose was hooked to my side like a Siamese twin.

I positioned my back to Melrose in an effort to get closer to Cynthia and create some privacy. Once the mood was right, I placed my hand on Cynthia's leg and gave her thigh a gentle rub. She responded by putting her hand on top of my mine. It was aggressive too! I felt like she was doing some subliminal voodoo shit to make sure my hand didn't move from her thigh. Not a chance.

We talked smack, drank and laughed all the way through dinner. I gazed at Cynthia the whole night. I was still looking for a bad angle but there wasn't one to be found. I didn't want the night to end and suggested that we go to my friend Lloyd's nightclub. As with the night before, I called my boys and brother Earl to join us. They were my safety net to break the fall in case anything went down that provoked Cynthia to kick me to the curb.

We entered the club through a VIP, back door entrance, where we bumped into Cee Lo Green. He was staring a pothole through Cynthia. I clutched her hand to let him know she was rolling with me. Cynthia laced her fingers tightly between mine, and for the first time I knew she was feeling me. I think I may have grabbed Melrose's hand too, *in a brotherly way.*

The rooftop was standing-room-only, so we found a spot to chill out on the second floor. I knew she was leaving the next morning and it felt like the night was moving in slow motion. I was taking in every detail about her. All I could see were her high cheekbones and those perfectly bowed lips that curled at the ends when she smiled. I needed to kiss her the first opportunity I got.

Before the thought could leave my mind, opportunity prevailed and I went right in to steal one. When I pulled away, she had a look of astonishment on her face that made me check myself. I felt like I was about to catch a brick in a club full of people. In my mind, I could already hear her shrieking, *"What the hell?"* Her mean mugging didn't crush my confidence, though. My chest was burning for more of her, and I quenched the heat with a second helping of her deliciousness. I must have misread her facial expression because that time, *she kissed me back.* I knew she wanted me all along.

It was a long shot for me to make a move on this ridiculously beautiful woman, but when she returned the gesture, I was reassured. It was then I knew the deal was officially closed. Throughout the rest of the night, I kept my hand on some part of her body, but always in a respectable place. I wanted her to know I was into her and there were a thousand possibilities that awaited us.

We left the club around two in the morning and between dinner and clubbing, we'd thrown back a small distillery. She was a little lit and immediately reclined her seat when she got into the truck. She threw those long legs up on the dashboard like she was posing for one of her sexy billboard ads. Unfortunately for me, her legs weren't the only raised body parts in the vehicle. I was having some serious biological changes with my third leg. Her short skirt hiked up to her cream-colored panties, coupled with an unintentionally suggestive posture, gave me a boner out of this world. My shit was crazy!

The 1990 Peter Thomas would've pulled over on the side of the road and tried to make something jump off, but I just watched her sleep the whole ride. The sight inspired me to turn what should have been a twenty-minute ride into forty-five minutes. I stared at her every stoplight, but I maintained my cool. I just knew this woman would one day be my wife, and I wasn't about to let a hard-on fuck it up.

When we reached Boris', I sat there admiring her beauty for a good minute before waking her. I didn't want her to catch me gawking, because I knew it would spook her out. Eventually, I nudged her softly until she opened her eyes. After walking her to the door and waiting until a light came on inside, I headed back to the truck. I immediately began thinking about picking her up later that Sunday morning. I was down to do everything in my power to make her mine.

Knowing that she had a mid-day flight back to New York, I called her early to request one last date. She answered the phone in an angelic, seductive, half-asleep voice. As I started forming the sentence to invite her to brunch, she accepted before I could finish, as if she knew the invitation was coming.

During brunch, she didn't flinch once when The Ritz-Carlton staff repeatedly addressed her as Mrs. Thomas. By the end of our meal, she'd been labeled with the Thomas brand at least a dozen times. *Baby girl was wearing it too.* Her face showed that she was trying it on to see how it fit and how it felt. She couldn't even play it off! She was made to wear the title, and I could feel that we were both down to take things in that direction.

I was already feeling lonely, knowing that we were only a ten-minute drive from the airport. It wasn't a trip I could stretch out because I didn't want her to miss her flight. When we reached the airport it felt like she'd just arrived hours before. I didn't want her to go. I wanted to kiss her really badly, but I was too spazzed out. It took everything I had to give her a hug and hold it together. As I watched her enter the airport, her butt cheeks were speaking my language as they shifted from side to side like they were performing an interpretive dance. I couldn't even front – I felt empty seeing her walk away. My supermodel jetted off like a superhero. *Damn, I forgot to ask her if she was still interested in selling me the truck.*

CHAPTER III

Frequent Flyer
Our Courtship

Cynthia's Emergency Deicing

EVEN AS MY plane touched down in New York, I was stupefied over how smitten with Peter I'd become during my visit to Atlanta. Shortly after landing at LaGuardia, I called to let him know I'd made it back safely. I was excited when he picked up after half a ring. We spoke my entire cab ride home. I wanted to talk longer but I was eager to relieve my nanny and spend some quality time with Noelle.

Returning to the familiar hustle and bustle of the city, I thought the spell of Peter would've diminished. However, being home only proved that something had transpired during my trip that had me losing my New York state of mind. For the first time, I started to see my once-perfect metropolis differently. The very city I'd always loved for its imperfections was now an island of flaws to me. The people didn't seem as nice as those in Atlanta. Georgians were completely at home with casually greeting strangers and striking up random conversations.

The streets of New York looked dirtier than what I'd remembered and traffic was a bitch. Atlanta was clean, filled with southern hospitality and seemed like an ideal place to raise a family. It's beautiful, spacious and affordable houses were another added benefit. Most importantly, it was home to the Jamaican gentleman I was apparently falling for. In the words of Ray Charles, Peter Thomas and Atlanta had *Georgia on my m*ind.

Later that night on the phone, Peter and I reflected on our weekend together. The time we shared had undoubtedly been significant for both of us. I could tell he'd started to genuinely care for me. He was opening up more and sharing personal things that he'd not revealed during my visit. He told me about the trials of his last relationship that had left him in a tailspin and living back home with his parents.

His living situation wasn't a deterrent for me, and it was refreshing seeing how much his mom and dad supported his entrepreneurial spirit. It was clear why he felt comfortable staying with them until he could regain financial traction. In a relationship, that type of circumstance was trivial and didn't bother me. If I liked a man – I liked him. I felt l knew Peter before I'd ever met him. The intersecting pathways in our lives had given me an inside track on his work ethic and determination. Everything about him convinced me that he was headed back to the top of his game.

For the next few weeks, we talked on the phone regularly. Our discussions were bottomless – sometimes lasting past four in the morning. Even if there was nothing substantial to talk about, we were content with simple phone banter. The topic of our next and much-anticipated rendezvous came up every time we spoke. Where would it be? New York? Atlanta? Miami? Admittedly, I was opposed to the idea of him visiting New York. I felt it was too soon for me to introduce him to Noelle, and it would've been weird for him to come and not meet her. One month after my trip to Atlanta, we finally agreed on the date and spot for my second *layover*. I booked a ticket and was heading back to the A-T-L.

On my first visit, the fact that Peter and I never discussed the sale of my truck was mint proof of my temporary insanity. Even though I was really digging Peter, I knew I'd like him more once we sealed the deal on the vehicle. I forced myself to complete our transaction as quickly as possible.

My personal feelings were bleeding into my business rationale, and the deeper I fell for him, the less comfortable I became with our negotiations. If I'd waited any longer, I would've probably given him the damn truck. Not really. *Well, maybe.* Before my return trip to Atlanta, we managed to agree on a price for the truck. He had his attorney draw up the paperwork and overnight the money. I was relieved to have the deal finally closed and eager to return to Atlanta to close other unfinished business.

I arrived in Atlanta on a bright Saturday morning. That time, *I flew pretty.* I was more comfortable, less nervous and undeniably ready for whatever the weekend had in store. Always the gentlemen, Peter offered to pick me up. Waiting for him outside the airport, things had already begun to feel surreal. I knew I wanted to spend as much time as possible with him, and there were no foreseeable obstacles standing in the way this time. I wasn't planning to kick it with a long-lost girlfriend or looking to sell a vehicle. This trip was all about Peter and getting to know him.

Peter had booked a hotel room for me in the city, and I initially believed he'd reserved it especially for me. I soon learned we'd be roommates that weekend. I didn't mind him being in tow because the three-day trip was strictly a strategic endeavor. I wasn't checking for a long-distance relationship, and I wanted to know if I was really into Peter (minus the shots of liquid courage). It was my turn at the wheel and I was more than ready to conduct *The Cynthia Bailey Inquisition*.

I needed to get into his headspace the way he'd trampled into mine like a rodeo bull on the loose. The mountain of curiosities he had about me, were now stirring in my head about him. Outside of the physical attraction, how did he really feel about me? What was the deal in the intimacy department? I knew he could give a soft peck on the lips, but could he bring the tongue action? I wasn't putting sex *on* the table like a buffet option, but I wasn't going to deny myself either. I was open to whatever curiosities needed to be satisfied and whatever temptations we unleashed.

He pulled up curbside at the airport, stuffed my bags in the truck and gave me a man-sized hug. I wanted to jump on him and hump him like a spider monkey, but I maintained my cool. It's my nature to never be the aggressor in a relationship. I enjoy allowing things to play out naturally, without limitations. I don't remember what Peter was wearing that day; I can only recall that he looked good. It seemed each encounter got better than the time before. He was morphing into an Idris Elba-Denzel Washington hybrid right before my eyes. I'd never been a woman to fall for a guy strictly over the physical. In my book, conversation and mental depth always trumped physicality.

Not more than five minutes into our ride, he asked if I'd mind stopping by the car wash with him. I thought, *"Oh hell, here we go again with his errand shit! Couldn't he have figured this out before I arrived? Why didn't he wash the damn car before picking me up?"* I simply wanted a hot meal and a freakin' cocktail. My wants aside, I appreciated a clean car and was easily sucked into Peter's carwash errand. He took the truck to one of those fancy, hand-wash places. While he gave the washers explicit instructions, I took a seat inside the deserted waiting room. I sat on a couch that looked like a recycled back-row seat that was stripped right out of the Partridge family van. When I saw the odd lobby seating, I smiled on the inside. I was coming to terms with the reality that Peter's aura attracted unusual, comical things.

He joined me in the waiting area, sat next to me and with no holds barred – proceeded to tongue me down. Truth be told, *we exploded on each other*. He was definitely getting *some* before Sunday. I had not had sex in almost a year and my conjugal interactions had strictly been with my little pink buddy who slept next to me (in the nightstand drawer). Even if Peter and I decided not to become an item, I was certain two epic things would happen as a result of my second trip to Atlanta – I was getting laid *and* double frequent flyer miles.

Leaving the carwash, Peter's carnivorous attack on me continued. It was pretty obvious we were both hungry, but not for food. Though I was starving and could've eaten, we passed two dozen restaurants and headed straight to the hotel. All the way there, we percolated, like two pots of water near boiling point. Being hit with the opportunity to have sex after so many months of celibacy, I recognized parts of my body had been asleep.

I guess I'd grown numb to how much I missed the foreplay and intimacy that preceded sex. Cell by cell, my hot pocket was awakening, and Peter was about to reap the benefit of all the life that was flooding back into it. He was just the one to break my dry spell. I knew by the way he kissed me that he was a grown man who could put down some mature loving. I was about to get some action and no gas station pit stop to buy batteries would be necessary!

Lead-footing it to the hotel, Peter almost ran every car within fifty feet off the road. I don't even think he put the truck in park when we arrived. He just jumped from behind the wheel, threw the key at the valet and made a bee-line for the lobby. It was my second trip to Atlanta, I hadn't been on the ground for an hour and I was already giving up the goodies. The only explanation I could offer is that there was a blazing fire in me that needed to be put out, and Peter was the fire chief on the scene. I felt like all eyes were on us and everybody knew we were about to have sex. We were as transparent as onion skin. Having gone without the sexual gratification of a man for such a long time, part of me felt I deserved a Weekend Hoe Pass.

There were no formalities once the door of our hotel room closed. Peter tossed our bags on the floor and started tearing me apart. It wasn't often in my life that I didn't overthink a situation, and that time was no exception. Even in the throes of passion, I wondered if I was making the right decision. Would he respect me the next day? Did I need an Altoid? Was I wearing matching underwear?

After our first round of intimacy was over, I felt like a caged bear that had been awakened from a long winter's nap. Everything felt perfectly normal. It wasn't until after the second (or third) helping that I was back to questioning my actions. What the hell had just happened? Was Peter going to leave money on the night table and be out? I was going one flew over the cuckoo's nest crazy! When he was still lying next to me an hour later, something told me all was well and he would still respect me in the morning. I allowed myself to be extra greedy and went back in for another round. That time, I was in full-floozy mode and made up my mind to be the best one to ever hit Atlanta.

After our extraordinary sexual intensity had been put to bed (*literally*), I could form intelligent sentences again. My mind was clear and all I could think about was having a nice meal and enjoying the next few days together. I'm a list girl, and from the time I'd landed in Atlanta, I'd been crossing things off a running tab in my head. I now had another item to scratch off, "*Have great sex with Peter.*" Done! Five stars. Exclamation point.

Peter's Emergency Deicing

Following Cynthia's first visit to Atlanta, we talked on the phone seven nights a week. More often than I could count, I woke up with the phone buried under me after dozing off. She would call me before, during, and after her photo shoots – and always after putting Noelle to bed. She relaxed me and it felt natural sharing intimate details about where I was in life – my kids, their moms, the build out of my new supper club – and where I eventually hoped to be.

Our phone courtship continued for four weeks, but my mind was always on putting her next visit on the calendar. She was hesitant about me coming to New York, so I invited her back to Atlanta. Since I was in the middle of building Uptown, the arrangement actually worked better for me. I was excited to have her all to myself the second time around. I truly liked Cynthia and prayed she was being as truthful with me as I'd been with her. I needed everything to work out for us because I wanted her bad! We'd had quite a few steamy conversations about our sexual likes and dislikes. Some made me tense, but I longed to see if I remembered her pleasure points and how everything would go down when we finally got busy.

On her return trip to Atlanta, I picked her up in what was officially my truck. As I cut the corner into the airport, she called to say she already had her bags and was waiting for me outside. Her voice sounded so pure. Young. Jubilant. Unencumbered. Pulling up, my eyes immediately caught sight of her long, shiny legs that filled up a pair of khaki shorts. All I could see was glistening skin. I remember thinking, "*Look at all that woman, and she got an ass too!*" Her beauty was criminal! I needed to meet her parents and see what they looked like. I just had to know the origin of all her crazy beauty. Her mama had to be fine as hell!

I was having all these thoughts as she stepped out from the curb and walked toward the truck. It was just a three-day visit, but her bag was twice as large as the one she'd brought before. This time around, she must've packed the whole damn mall in her suitcase. But nothing mattered to me more than her finally being in the same city with me. I grabbed her big-ass bag, gave her a hug and opened her door. Her lips were shining like she had glossed them down with Armor All. They looked outrageously succulent. I wanted to stare at her the whole time I was driving, but I had to check myself before I hit something *or somebody*. I felt like the luckiest man on the planet. She'd come back to see me (and only me).

In preparation of her arrival, I had been running around and didn't have time to clean the truck. I asked if she would mind stopping by the car wash, and she graciously agreed. I felt like she was digging me to the point that she would have gone to the moon with me on a bicycle. It was only around eleven in the morning, and I needed to kill some time until her hotel room was ready. I figured it was a practical move that couldn't hurt. The place was slow that day, and Cynthia and I lucked out having the whole inside waiting room to ourselves.

I was wearing a white V-neck T-shirt, jeans and flip-flops. Standing barefoot next to each other, I stood an inch taller than Cynthia. However, in her stilettos and my flip-flops, she towered a clean four inches over me. I wasn't trying to be standing up under her looking like Kevin Hart, so I took a seat beside her and *went in*. I kissed her like a beast and she kissed me back, ferociously. The flavored Armor All on her lips tasted as delicious as it looked, and kissing her was like a dream (come true). It was exactly how I thought it would be, ***perfect.***

We kissed for about twenty minutes. I felt like my pants were going to blow up. I was a grown-ass man making out in a carwash like a teenager at a drive-in theater. There was mad passion shooting through my whole body. I hadn't had sex that meant something to me in over two years, but I was about to be all in with Cynthia. I knew it wasn't just the physical with her, and it made me feel like a scared boy on the inside. I didn't want to disappoint her sexually or otherwise.

We had plans to go to dinner, but decided to bypass the burritos and get straight to the booty call. *There was no way in hell I was gonna sit in a restaurant for two hours with that boner.* Nor did I want to risk losing the sensation and rawness of the moment. I knew if my shit was crazy, hers had to be ridiculous. We both agreed that the hotel was the only possible next stop. I kissed her at every stoplight and kept my free hand plastered on her thigh. I couldn't get to that room fast enough.

I'd stopped by the hotel before picking her up to do an early check in and pick up the room key. We took the elevator straight to the penthouse and as soon as our feet touched the carpet, *it was on*. I backed her up against the door and held her hostage. By the time we'd passionately stumbled to the bed, not more than four feet away, we were both buck naked. I knew exactly what she was referring to when she asked if I had "something." I was quick to whip out a condom to show her that I would not only be a great lover but also a responsible one. I went at her like a champion and she received it *like a championette.*

She was perfect and everything I'd ever wanted. When I made love to her, I felt like I was dreaming. I found myself saying everything a man would say while making love to a woman he loved. After two or three ravenous bouts, I got up to take a shower. While I was under the water she called out, "Peter?" I yelled back, "What?" She said, "I love you." I froze. Did she say she loved me? After a solid minute, I asked back, "Really? You do?" She assertively confirmed my question. I was shocked. The moment felt unreal. Was it possible? Could she actually be in love with me? I didn't know if it was the loving I'd put down or what. I knew it was good, but damn!

From the way she touched me when we made love, I believed her. I knew my life had just changed. Making love to her was the point of no return and an unspoken pact that neither of us wanted to be with anyone else. Even though I hadn't returned her revelation, Cynthia and I were indisputably in love with each other. The sex was off the charts and we were past the formalities. No discussion was necessary – *Cynthia was going to be my wife*. This wasn't random sex between two people, and I felt it was time she considered relocating to Atlanta.

Cynthia's One-Way Ticket

Telling Peter I loved him was submitting to my uncontrollable urge to let him know how I felt. I had to speak the words or I was going to burst. Looking back, it was also one of my subconscious methods of testing him. From experience, I knew that a man hearing those three little words after a first sexual encounter would either get a rise in his pants or shit in them. I wrestled with my inner self, waiting to see which Peter would prove to be.

He was definitely good in bed and it had been scientifically proven that we were sexually compatible. The intimacy placed a different level of focus on the relationship for me. I wanted things to be serious and exclusive between us. My typical behavior wasn't to fly into a city, have sex with a guy

I'd officially met twice and throw up deuces. That wasn't my style. I could only hope Peter felt the same, but I wasn't sure. Besides, I wasn't about to be flying back and forth to Atlanta every month on a weekend booty pass. I could get sex all day long in New York and didn't need to get on a plane to get my rocks off.

My goal was to end the trip with a mutual agreement that we were more than cut buddies. My inner voice told me the way he'd turned me inside out, it wasn't *just sex* for Peter. Everything just felt so right, and I was game to go with the flow of the weekend. Anything that felt that damn good had to be going somewhere. I stayed centered, promised myself I'd be honest about everything and laid back for the ride. *Pun intended.*

When you turn forty, you lose the luxury of time. It's a sobering reality that forces you to separate the shit that's real from the shit that ain't. I knew Peter was real because he made me feel safe. In a perfect world, I would have liked for things to have transitioned slower between us. Everything in our courtship seemed to have moved at breakneck speed, and I felt powerless to stop it.

Originally, I'd gone to Atlanta on a weekend excursion to sell my truck, but got hooked on this dude instead. A month later I went back, we did the nasty and I told him I loved him the first time. More terrifying, the madness wasn't over! Peter had me contemplating the thought of uprooting my daughter and life in New York for a move to Atlanta. Then, twenty-four hours after Peter and I made love for the first time, he took me to meet his parents. WHOA!

It never crossed my mind that I'd meet Peter's mother and father during that trip. His urgency for me to meet them before I left was just as brazen as my confession of love to him. It was the ultimate sign that he wanted to be in it with me for the long haul. Though neither of us verbalized it, I left Atlanta that weekend knowing I was Peter's woman. I headed home to initiate the process of Operation Shutdown. I was on a mission to tie up all my loose dating ends back in New York. There weren't any serious suitors, but a few hopefuls that needed to be pink-slipped. I wanted to concentrate all my energy on the likelihood of a future with Peter.

Several anxiety-filled weeks after my second visit to Atlanta, I got up the nerve to invite Peter to New York. It only made sense for him to stay at my home during his visit. We'd already slept together, and making him check into a hotel would have been a waste of valuable time. I wanted to wake up next to him each morning and spend every possible moment together. I was also confident in showing him what I looked like in the morning on my own turf.

I discussed his visit with Noelle's father, because I knew Peter would be meeting our daughter. Leon grilled me with all the questions a doting, protective father would be expected to have. It wasn't a hard sell. He trusted my judgment and knew if I was comfortable bringing a man around our daughter, that person had to be upright. Sharing Peter's impending visit was more of a courtesy than a request for permission, because I didn't have anything to prove to anyone. I was an adult, it was my house and I paid the rent. Without question, Peter would be staying there.

There was just one other small issue I needed to iron out. Small as in eight years old, but hardly a matter I considered little. In fact, this was a giant issue. Noelle had her own bedroom, but had slept in my bed since she was a baby. She wasn't exactly thrilled at the prospect of resigning her post, and it was hard to explain this new man that had popped into my life. I never brought random men around my daughter, but for the right man (and Peter was), I made it a priority to explain my decision on a level Noelle could understand.

I told her I'd met someone that I really liked and he was coming from out of town to see me. Noelle had never witnessed me give anyone else the type of attention I usually reserved solely for her. I knew Peter's visit would be a definite adjustment. She seemed pretty accepting of it all until I got to the part about him staying at our place and sleeping in my bed. She was all too happy to offer up her room as a sleeping option for Peter.

I gently explained that adults who like each other usually sleep in the same bed. Translation: *she wouldn't be sleeping with mommy during Peter's stay.* The decision was ultimately mine to make, not my eight-year-old daughter's. Anyway, it was a perfect time to break the cycle and start weaning Noelle from my bed. After all, one day she would be going away to college and I probably wouldn't be her roommate.

It was a luxury to step right into Peter's car, curbside at Atlanta's Jackson Hartsfield Airport, but folks didn't get picked up from the airport in New York. Being a New Yorker himself, Peter knew the ropes and took a taxi to my apartment. It couldn't have worked out any better, because I wanted to use the extra time to reassure Noelle. This was a different experience for her, yet I could tell she was curious to meet Peter. Noelle loved her dad and was at an age where she often questioned why we weren't together. She was a typical, outspoken, charismatic New York kid who would've replaced Peter with her dad in a heartbeat.

When Peter finally arrived at our home and I introduced them, she was polite but very reserved. She basked in the opportunity to get me alone and ask why my new boyfriend was so old. I believe her exact words were, "He's nice Mommy, but he's an old man." I explained that Peter and I were just a few years apart in age. She challenged my explanation by asking why Peter had a gray beard if he wasn't old. I laughed hysterically on the inside, but fell short of finding the right words to answer her logical question.

Peter and I took Noelle on a trip to the zoo, and afterwards I conveniently dropped her off for a sleepover at her friend's house. Returning home without Noelle felt unsettling, but Peter had a way about him that relaxed me. I loved watching him in my home. He acted so comfortable, *like he was supposed to be there.* Something about being in Atlanta made what we shared feel like a fantasy. New York was my home, and now it was all starting to feel real for me. It was really my life, Peter was really there with me and he'd met the most important person in my world, Noelle.

We were very much into each other and our union was quite natural. Peter was never shy about sharing his feelings with me. He used every opportunity to bring up the topic of me relocating to Atlanta. In all honesty, I had reached a point in my career where I didn't have to be in New York to work. The more I was with Peter, the more I felt like I'd *been there, done that* with New York. I'd experienced the VIP scene, spent the summers in the Hamptons, traveled the world and been exposed to so many outlooks, cultures and people. Peter was absolutely right when he said it was time to cross New York off my mental to-do list.

Do the damn thing in New York City?

Check!

Peter's One-Way Ticket

Cynthia's second trip to Atlanta was only for three days. I had a lot of ground to cover before her departure. I showed her my Uptown project and we spent time driving around and looking at homes. I wanted her to know my taste and offer her a glimpse of what life with me in Atlanta would look like. It was important for me to establish a standard before she boarded that plane back home. I was serious as high blood pressure about this woman.

I kept telling myself to tread the waters lightly, but in my heart I was putting all my hopes out into the universe. My attention slowly shifted to figuring out her transition from up north to down south. We weren't spring chickens, and I wasn't about to play house with Cynthia. As badly as I wanted to share the same space with her, my lack of income would prevent her from moving immediately. With Macy's in New York being a huge chunk of her modeling work, she had more of a financial cushion than I did. Still, we both agreed she would be the one to relocate, since my restaurant build-out required that I stay in Atlanta. After leaving my ex in South Florida, I was in a phase of reinventing myself. It was a fragile time. I was on a mission to adequately provide for my five biological kids, the eventual addition of Cynthia as my new wife *and her child*. I put on my game face, focused on getting Uptown opened and the paper flowing.

Cynthia was a healthy distraction that kept me focused and motivated. On her second trip to Atlanta, I can't explain why it was so important for me to introduce her to my parents, particularly my father. I didn't grow up feeling close to him because he worked a lot, but he'd always been present for the big moments in my life. He watched me struggle with being a young father of two children in my first marriage. Then, he bailed me out of a dark place when promiscuity ended my relationship with the mother of my third child. We never married after she had our daughter, but she was an upright woman who deserved more than I gave. During our relationship, my unquenchable thirst for women got the best of me. She ordered me to get the hell out of her life when my fourth child was conceived with a one-night stand.

As with all my previous relationships, my dad had a front-row seat to the devastating breakup with my fifth child's mother. I was in Atlanta, while she was living in Miami with our son. She wasn't speaking to me or allowing me to see our son as often as I wanted. It was a bunch of silly bullshit that had my moods swinging on a pendulum, waking up mad and going to bed sad – or vice versa. I was constantly trying to find ways to block out the pain. Where I was concerned, my dad had seen it all!

My exchange with women paralleled his struggles with fidelity. He fathered four children outside of his forty-something-year marriage to my mother. I guess it's true that we become the things we hate most in life. He was my father and I would not have replaced him with anything in the world – but I never wanted to be like him in that way. Deep down inside I always felt he understood me on a level no one else could.

All my life, it had been difficult for me to discuss my dad without becoming emotional. He never said it, but I'd always felt like he didn't achieve what he dreamed for his life. When his parents died young, he took on the responsibility of raising his nine brothers and four sisters. He had a grit that ultimately made him more financially successful than any of them, but he wasn't happy.

Growing up, I witnessed him coming home drunk on the regular. He was never abusive and only physically disciplined me twice in my life. My mother did the physical chastising, but my dad could give a verbal lashing that felt like an old-fashioned ass whooping. He wasn't mean-spirited in his punishment. He just had a way of talking that made you feel bad and never want to make the same mistake twice.

My father was a carpenter by trade. His daily routine consisted of rising at three in the morning, returning home from work around four in the afternoon and repeating the same shit the next day. Sometimes his work-week would include the weekend, and he would take my younger brother Earl and me along. I held a deep reverence for the struggles and sacrifices that I saw him suffer. I can still remember the day our youngest brother was struck by a car and killed. I was only fifteen years old. The pain of his death was forever etched in my parents' faces, especially my dad's. I really felt for him.

Losing my baby brother destroyed a part of him, while the monotony of his daily grind slowly chipped away at what was left. He worked hard, never abandoned his children and was always present in a broken kind of way. Providing for his family seemed to be the only happiness in his life. It would not have been a stretch to say he was depressed. He numbed his frustration and pain with an intoxicating cocktail of alcohol and women. I could always smell the overpowering scent of his unhappiness. I guess it's why I never judged him for having children outside of his marriage to my mother. At the end of the day, I was just a kid who loved his dad.

My mother was a strong woman who could have left and made it on her own if she had wanted. When they married, she brought along two daughters from a previous relationship. He cared for both girls and raised them as his own. I've always believed my mom stayed because she saw in him all the same things I did. She knew he was an imperfect man, but she loved him completely.

My dad paid twenty-six years of apartment rent to his Brooklyn landlord, Mr. Stern, but never experienced the satisfaction of New York homeownership. In all his wrongs, there was always something monumental about him that outshined his mistakes. That's why I loved him so hard, but his agony was painted all over me like a cheap suit. It made me something I didn't want to be, and I hit the streets selling major drugs at twenty-four years old. When I finally left the hood, it was long overdue. I knew the only way I could lift the suffocating pressure of my father's pain was to get the hell out of dodge.

I knew my father supported me making good decisions and wanted me to find the right woman. He witnessed the massive bullshit I endured in my five-year relationship before Cynthia. He knew I put everything (emotionally and financially) into helping that woman establish her business and a solid life. He offered nothing less than encouragement by allowing me to move back home for the first time since I was eighteen. When I realized Cynthia was *the one,* I had to show her off immediately. She would be my proof to him that I wasn't going to mess up again.

My dad wasn't home the day I took Cynthia to meet my parents. I drove to a south-side barbershop where my mom told me I would find him. He thought I was crazy for hunting him down. I'd never gone looking for my father for anything in my life, nor brought a woman home to meet him. *He knew it was a crucial matter.* I believed my actions made him fall in love with Cynthia on the spot, and I could sense Cynthia was resolved in some new way after meeting him.

I'd exposed all my vulnerabilities to Cynthia that weekend, and she left Atlanta knowing my every soft spot. I needed her to know who I was and that I wasn't hiding any secrets. She was responsive. The more I gave, the more she seemed to want. When the time came to drop her off at the airport on Tuesday afternoon, we vowed to see each other at least once a month and make it work no matter what. Whatever making "it" work looked like and whatever demands came along – we were prepared to do it. It was clear to me that she wanted us to be partners and take on the world together.

Her only hesitation was putting herself in a situation where she wouldn't be Noelle's sole provider. Cynthia Bailey wasn't the type of woman to wait on a child support check to take care of her kid. She wasn't afraid to work, and wouldn't think of dragging a man into court to make him man up to his responsibilities. This was a woman who'd given Jayson Williams back his engagement ring. She broke it off with him while he was at the height of his NBA career and sitting on a one-hundred-million dollar contract. She was the fearless female who told record mogul Russell Simmons it wasn't the right time for her to accept his marriage proposal. Cynthia had even walked away from her daughter's father while he was a rising Hollywood heartthrob.

She didn't base the future of her relationships on money or fame. It was always about her authentic happiness and being in a position to provide for herself and Noelle. Any outside support was a cherry on her sundae, but she wasn't the one to be standing on a curb with a begging hand held out. She was the kind of woman I wanted to roll with *for life*. My chest swelled at the thought of knowing I had the chance to prove myself and earn her respect. She was so worth it.

Cynthia's Upgrade

With Uptown being only months away from its grand opening, it would not have made sense for Peter to move to New York. I didn't know a lot about Georgia, but I'd always been one for making a change, as long as it didn't stifle my ability to have a career or make a living. When the time came to transition to Atlanta, I was mentally and financially prepared. Peter, on the other hand, seemed a little jolted the day we landed at his doorstep. Even though he had long anticipated our arrival, it was still an adjustment for him. We rolled up like a hurricane in a windmill, and his place was transformed in a span of twenty-four hours. Noelle, the nanny and I converted his swank bachelor's condo into a modest single-family home in the blink of an eye.

It didn't take long for him to start acting funny – coming home looking at me sideways with major attitude. I wasn't having it on *no* level! I knew damn well this man didn't have me displace my entire life to start having second thoughts after the deed was already done. It wasn't like I stuffed the contents of my life into a U-Haul, drove to Atlanta and called him from a payphone asking, "Guess who's here?" Peter was very much a part of my move and every logistical decision. I was disappointed and pissed off by his behavior.

I knew some of his energy was directed toward my nanny. It was difficult for him to understand that she was a necessity, not an extravagance. Noelle was my top priority and her nanny was like a second mother. Being with her was like being with me. Their closeness was a bond that would've made most women insecure. *Not me.* Noelle's nanny had been with me since her birth, and when I had my baby I felt like she had one too. My work and travel schedule was hectic and erratic. Her presence helped me feel more grounded about leaving my child for an assignment. Noelle needed to be taken care of, and the nanny was there to heed her every beck and call.

Needless to say, she was as much a part of my package deal as Noelle (and her daddy). From the beginning, I put all my cards on the table. I knew it was a lot of shit and moving pieces for any man to juggle, but no conditions in my life should have come as a surprise to Peter. As much as I loved him, if Noelle, the nanny and I were cramping his style, I was prepared to call the moving company and work out a two-for-one deal to get my ass back to Manhattan. Noelle was my supreme deal breaker, and all bets were off where she was concerned. If the world wasn't right with her, it wasn't right with me. If the world wasn't right with me ... *Houston, we gotta problem!*

Peter's place was always intended to be a temporary solution, not a permanent home to raise a family. Even before my move, he had his sights set on the house where we now live. I never laid eyes on it until I got to Atlanta, but I knew it would be suitable for Noelle from the pictures Peter sent. The pictures showcased a neighborhood that resembled a little Hamptons of the South, with people walking their dogs and riding bikes. The house itself was the perfect size, having enough bedrooms and space for the nanny and overnight guests. I thought it was great and saw no reason not to move forward. Peter had visited my apartment in New York, and I was convinced he understood my taste. More importantly, I knew he had meticulously chosen the home with us in mind, and I trusted his sensibilities.

Once we settled into our new home, all was well. I found a great school for Noelle, Peter had more room and the nanny was happy. Uptown was thriving and so was my career. I was forty years old and had no plans of completely forfeiting my modeling checks, but I was very open to a career change. As my personal priorities began to shift, traveling back and forth for work grew more stressful. For the first time in my life, I started to consider a professional move outside of modeling. I was on a hunt to find a gig that would keep me in Atlanta more and traveling less.

Peter's Upgrade

Uptown opened its doors on New Year's Eve, 2007. Cynthia flew in for the grand opening party and had Boris and Nicole lend their names to promote the event. The following February, I threw a blowout birthday bash for Cynthia, and she came back to town with all her famous friends from New York. That time marked a year of us dating and alternating visits between New York and Atlanta. I was over the long-distance dating thing and wanted to live in the same city with my woman.

Searching through communities I knew she would like, I found a house that had our names written all over it! I emailed her pictures of the home's interior and exterior, and she agreed it was the right place for us to start our lives. Even though it would be a sight unseen decision for Cynthia, I steamrolled ahead in setting up the purchase. She appreciated my flavor for the finer things and insisted that my approval was enough to make her secure in moving forward. It was hard to put in words how *extra-ordinary* her unconditional trust made me feel.

Month-to-month leases didn't exist in New York. You either initiated a new full-term lease or got the hell out. Unfortunately, Cynthia's lease expired before our home was completed, so once we signed the purchase contract I didn't drag my feet in getting her to Atlanta. We started the process of securing financing and setting up the closing. I paid off a $20,000 balance on one of her credit cards, and we used her credit to secure our mortgage. She couldn't pack up and get to stepping fast enough.

Our makeshift plan was that we'd all live in my 1,000 square foot, two-bedroom condo until the house was ready. In June of 2008, my residence became home base for the three of us *and Noelle's nanny.* I was cool with Cynthia and Noelle being in my tiny place, but the addition of the nanny was throwing me off! I just couldn't get past the fact that there was another grown-ass stranger living in my crib. She was a nice lady, but at the end of the day, she wasn't going home at five o'clock. When nightfall came, she was sleeping on the other side of the wall where Cynthia and I got busy.

Cynthia could sense I was feeling some type of way and it started to annoy her. She thought my energy was projected at her and Noelle – nothing could have been further from the truth. My mindset was simply that I'd fallen in love with Cynthia and her daughter, the nanny wasn't in my equation. I just needed the solitude and square footage of a bigger place *and the nanny out of my grill!*

I never shared the real lowdown with Cynthia, because this nanny lady had been a part of their lives for years. Back then, Noelle was eight and homegirl was still in the picture. It was hard for Cynthia to function without her support. I wasn't stupid; I knew it was a three-piece meal with no substitutions. The breast, wing and biscuit were all one deal. I just shut the fuck up and went out of my way to make everyone comfortable until the move could happen.

When that day finally came, my condo was bursting at the seams with toys, fashion magazines, *the nanny* and shit everywhere! The nanny went along for the ride to the new house, but only stayed another year. She was gone by the time Noelle turned nine. Not at my urging, *of course.*

Having Noelle in my everyday home life was refreshing and something I was already familiar with. In my last relationship, I was the proud surrogate father to a daughter my ex had from a prior relationship. Though her dad was present and very involved in her life, I happily played the role of second dad. I loved her dearly, but the breakup with her mom was also the end of our bond. I had completely accepted her as my child and made the same sacrifices for her that I did for my own children. I swore I'd never get mixed up with another woman who came with a plus one. I didn't mind breaking up with the woman if we weren't jiving, but breaking up with the child was like pouring alcohol on hemorrhoids.

It was interesting to see all the places where the separation from my children had created issues in other parts of my life. One time in particular, I had visited Cynthia in New York and left feeling like she would hate me forever. Noelle had asked me to play with her, and I told her I didn't play board games with children. It was a time when I was hurting and longing to spend time with my young son in Miami. I wasn't thinking about the jab of my words or how they might hurt Noelle's feelings. Cynthia was quick to let me know if something like that happened again, we'd be toast.

Noelle has always been Cynthia's everything. Back then and even more so now, she's very guarded about her. When Cynthia and I moved in together, both sides of Noelle's family (her grandparents especially) were very protective and involved in our everyday lives. There was also the pressure of Noelle being the only child of a famous movie star – *and a daughter at that.* Leon was so influential in Noelle's life that Cynthia made me meet him before I could spend the night at her place that first time I visited New York. Everything regarding that child's life was a production. If she had even a cold, the world would stop! I always felt like too many hands were in the cookie jar.

Cynthia would not leave Noelle alone with me when she traveled for work. The nanny always had to be there. Though our relationship had a rocky start, I eventually took refuge in the nanny's presence. I learned she was a necessary buffer in my home life and relationship with Cynthia. If anything ever went down, she could stand witness for me against all the protecting arms around Noelle.

I had to constantly check my reactions to Cynthia's and the other adults' care of Noelle. I recognized that putting her first was really how it was supposed to be. Cynthia was a remarkable mother who would never make a decision that was not in the best interest of her daughter. Her outlook on things matter to me, and I grew to use her logic in weighing important decisions in my own life. She could only make me a better man, husband and father.

I wanted the world to see my diamond and it wouldn't be long before it got the opportunity. Just prior to her move to Georgia, Cynthia met a memorable black guy at a political fundraiser at L.A. Reid's house. She was so impressed by his intelligence and conversation that she had her money on him to win the seat he was running for. Months later, he beat out Hillary Clinton for the Democratic presidential nomination. That suave gentleman Cynthia had been so enthusiastic about was Barack Obama.

Her instinct about him was spot-on! In October 2008, he was elected the forty-fourth president of the United States of America. It was a powerful and exciting time for blacks everywhere, but the country was growing unstable. We were all in the chokehold of a crazy recession and just about every socioeconomic class was bracing for a beating. The country was changing, and our lives were also about to have a huge *reality* shift.

In Jan 2009, Satchel Jester, who handled marketing for Uptown, mentioned he'd caught whiff of a casting call for an Atlanta-based reality show. Its producers were apparently looking for an ambitious, self-made, African American woman. Satchel knew the casting director and mentioned to her that he thought Cynthia would be a great fit. I believed television was the best way for Cynthia to open herself up to greater opportunities, so I shared the proposition with her.

Other than what Satchel had told me, I knew nothing about the show or its cast. What I did know was Cynthia was a woman who had blindsided me with her beauty, poise, charm and class. If she had that effect on a tough guy like me, she could blow away any television audience. I arranged for her to meet with a woman by the name of April Love. April was helping with the casting for a show called *The Real Housewives of Atlanta (RHOA)*.

Cynthia's Upgrade (Part II)

Several months after moving into our new house, I stopped by Uptown to have lunch with Peter. His promotions coordinator struck up a conversation that completely threw me for a loop. He mentioned that his close friend was a casting agent for *The Real Housewives of Atlanta*. He went on to say that he had put a feather in her cap about me being a prospect for the upcoming third season. I couldn't wrap my brain around the concept and didn't think much of the exchange. That conversation with Satchel had been completely erased from my brain until Peter came home the following week and ran the idea by me again.

I was like hell to the naw! I was tripping that Peter was even seriously stepping to me about some reality TV hustle. I had never thought about doing reality TV and certainly not in a forum that featured six other women. Yes, I was at a crossroad in my career, but Peter's option was not a detour that registered on my GPS. Everything I knew about reality TV was enough to make me not want to know more. It didn't seem very progressive or favorable of a black woman's image. If I ever considered working in television, it would be supermodel Tyra Banks' blueprint that I'd use to make my transition from modeling. I'd always hoped that life after the runway would be fashion-related and saw no direct correlation between my current world and the reality world.

My gays were faithful RHOA fans and hounded me about the show's need for my character type. Their badgering was a flashback of how I got started in modeling. People would always walk up to me on the street and say, "You should be a model!" The message kept coming to me from every corner of my life until I answered the call. Now, I could see the same cosmic trend with RHOA. First Peter's promoter, then my gays and now there was an opportunity for me to actually sit down with April. Truthfully, Peter got on my nerves so bad, I really only agreed to a lunch meeting with April just to shut him up!

At lunch, I had my laundry list of questions prepared – each specific and to the point. How would I be compensated? Would the cameras be in our home 24/7, watching us sleep? How many days a week would I have to shoot? I had so many questions. April was not only direct in her answers, but gifted in piquing my interest. I went from hell to the naw, to *why the hell not*?

Though more receptive than I was before our meeting, I still wasn't completely sold on the idea. I couldn't see how I'd fit into the cast. I wasn't a messy person, I didn't hang out with bitchy, gossipy women and my life wasn't brimming with drama. How would I be an asset to the show with my no-drama storyline?

The modeling world had a lot of cattiness, but the battles were more about becoming the hot face of the moment. There was maliciousness as with any job, but it was an industry where you kicked it with the crew that matched your morals and flow. Nobody really had time for a hate agenda. There was an unspoken, mutual respect that was hardly ever broken and certainly not publicly. I was accustomed to being around women who were fabulous, but didn't advertise it. In fashion, women like Beverly Johnson simply wore it like a second skin. I could never have disrespected or talked shit on a set about Beverly. She was a matriarch who'd opened doors for women of color to model all over the world and have fruitful careers. The profession had instilled a modesty in me that probably wouldn't bolster show ratings.

I didn't want to invest a lot of energy into something that wasn't right for me. By way of casting, RHOA would put me in a situation where my friends would be chosen for me. I saw it as my biggest challenge because I wasn't cut from the same cloth as some of the women. However, April maintained that the show wanted a woman who was cosmopolitan, well-traveled but down to earth. Translation: *They were looking for a girl who enjoyed caviar and champagne, but wouldn't turn her nose up at neck bones and sweet tea.*

April said the show's viewers were more interested in seeing self-made, black women who had achieved success through their own sweat and merit, rather than those who married into money. In response, producers were looking to feature a complementary housewife profile in the third season. I still wrestled with how I could make a significant contribution while being me and staying true to my values.

I had a variety of restrictions that I felt made me a less-appealing addition. I wasn't going to cuss, fight or gratuitously flaunt my daughter on camera. In fact, I was only willing to show Noelle in relevant scenes, like ones including her father. April noted my concerns and submitted me for consideration to the powers that be. I was shocked to hear back that they liked me! Maybe my no-drama swagger would be the new style.

My meeting with April had my wheels turning nonstop. I started to think that for the right amount of money, I could figure the shit out. I began watching the show and familiarizing myself with all the ladies. The producers arranged an off-camera meeting between me and NeNe Leakes. My guess was they wanted to get a second opinion of me. I thought NeNe was the realest and funniest of the group, but also the one I would get along with the least. I saw myself hitting it off best with Kandi Burruss.

NeNe had a powerful presence that grabbed people's attention, but her appeal was quite different from mine. I was used to walking into a room and getting attention for my outfit, makeup and style. NeNe carried herself with a boldness and presence that you could not ignore. Her persona screamed, *"I have arrived!"* In her high heels, she stood an intimidating 6'3". Her confidence alone was enough to shift the energy in any room she entered.

I'd not met anyone like NeNe before. I thought I had a lot of charisma, but mine was about as bright as the sun at midnight in her company. From the first time I met her, I knew she was going to be a star. I was intrigued by her and understood how others could be sucked in too. She came across as a smart, assured woman with a plan. NeNe was the whole package and big in every way: size, personality, height and humor.

I remember thinking, even if I didn't join the cast, I was new to Atlanta and she would be a fun girl to hang out with. She was resourceful and could tell you how to get anything. Even if it was something she hadn't personally experienced, NeNe was that girl who had the 411 on where to get a great facial, perfect pedicure or a firm set of implants. I thought she was cool, but at the time I didn't feel the admiration was mutual. I knew she liked me and thought I was nice, but it's hard to get my disposition in the first five minutes of meeting me. I have to warm up to people. I was sure she didn't see me as a fit for the show. I even convinced myself that her feedback to the producers was pretty much just that.

I was told that the next step would be a screen test, but the Bravo calls fizzled after my face-to-face with NeNe. The lack of communication kicked me into proactive mode, and I turned the tables on the pursuit. I phoned the producers and told them they'd be making a big mistake not to at least audition me. A week later, camera crews were in my home.

The producers were seeking a housewife who women could watch as a means of escape from their everyday lives. They wanted women to look at the RHOA cast and think, *"Wow, I want that life."* Partaking in reality TV for the first time, the only instruction manual you have as a guide is what other cast members portray. I focused on emulating their behavior, thinking it was what I needed to bring to the show.

I went into the screen test very conflicted, battling with who I truly was, versus what I thought the show wanted me to be. I was so out of my element and hated sitting in front of a camera bragging about my life. It felt so silly and pompous. The producers prodded me to talk about the men I'd dated, the money I'd made, the places I'd traveled and people I'd rubbed shoulders with. If I was to become a Bravo Housewife, passing the screen test was the first order of business. It all clicked for me the moment I realized I could just give the producers what they needed and bring the balance to my character once I was cast for the show. After my epiphany, the rest was as effortless as walking down a runway.

I'd heard producers were looking for only one new housewife for the up-coming season. Word around town was that an Atlanta attorney Phaedra Parks was in the final running with me. I had never heard of her before the show, but knew we could not have been more different from each other. I got the impression that whoever had the best storyline would become a housewife and the other would be kept on as a cast mate, *if that.* A cast mate is anyone appearing on the show that doesn't hold a peach in the opening credits. I was claiming my peach and from that point on, I viewed Phaedra as my competition. Fortunately, each of us had unique contributions to offer, and the producers loved our storylines. She had a baby, I had a wedding, and we were both invited back to Season 4.

CHAPTER IV

Fasten Your Seatbelts
Our Reality Show

Peter's Lost & Found

I WAS HAPPY TO help Cynthia create an income for herself outside of modeling. She did a lot of print and television work for Macy's and was well-loved by its entire divisional team. Her bestselling ads were the reason her professional relationship with Macy's spanned over twenty years. Cynthia was more than a beautiful face; she had a skill and patience that made the job look easier than it was. Watching her do the same walk a dozen times (just to get the right angle) showed a mechanical side to modeling that not everyone is aware of. On one of my visits to her set, I was blown away to learn that it took forty-something people to make a single shoot come together. Everything was unionized: one group drove the truck, one unloaded it, another did audio and a team of about ten producers oversaw the whole setup.

When the recession hit, Macy's reduced its workforce around the country and closed most of the divisional catalog production studios. The majority of that work was moved to the main headquarters in New York. Macy's was one of Cynthia's regular gigs and the reductions were a big financial hit for her. My wife is a woman whose emotions are controlled by her finances. It was tough to watch her wrestle with whether she'd be able to survive the restructure. When RHOA came up, she wasn't hyped about the opportunity, but that was the only clear move on the chessboard. It was a *take it or leave it* situation. *I convinced her to take it.*

I know how to parlay shit, and I'm 100 percent guilty of being Cynthia's hype-man. I persuaded her that she had what it took to be a *Real Housewives* star. I had no doubt it would be the perfect outlet to showcase her greatness. The show wanted a fresh face and new blood to play off some of the circus-like personalities already on board. There was already a lot of ghetto cussing, wine drinking and wig snatching going on. Cynthia wasn't a woman to get caught up in excessive mess or gossip, and NeNe clearly detected that in their first meeting. However, Cynthia's fate was in the hands of the blue suits in charge, not any particular cast member. NeNe was already doing her thing – Cynthia just needed a chance to do hers. When weeks had gone by without word from Bravo, I encouraged Cynthia to personally contact them and follow up. She called the producers and assured them she would be worth their time.

She was a humble woman who never needed to toot her own horn. The whole notion of bragging about her life caused her to clam up during her test. A producer on set that day had coincidentally followed Cynthia's career and knew of her lavish lifestyle. He pulled her aside and told her straight up, "Look, Cynthia, you're a part of fashion and entertainment's *Who's Who*. I need you to show that and be that! You've been all around the world in private jets and been a guest to the prince of Morocco. *You're the woman we're looking for.*" Cynthia listened, stepped up her game and landed the part.

Once the deal was officially inked, we started watching DVDs of previous seasons in preparation for our first. What she saw turned her off even more than she'd been after sitting down with April. Cynthia's background and temperament didn't match any of the women. I had to resell her on the fact that she didn't have to come off like the other women. I told her she could make a mark of her own.

She was a multicultural woman who had a career and storyline that wasn't predictable. She was a breed that viewers could learn more interesting things about with each episode. Producers were also excited to show the contrasting dynamic of Cynthia's subtle side against my explosive side. They knew I didn't mince words or feel the need to appear perfect. They liked how her laid-back elegance bounced off my crazy Jamaican, Brooklyn swagger.

Our first season was financially and emotionally one of the worst times of my life. Every detail in our world was being played out on national television. Being me on the daily was already a freaking television show in itself, but joining RHOA was one I never saw coming. I struggled to get used to crews filming at our home and Uptown. Talking on camera about my children and four baby mamas was the real kick in the ribs. Not having my kids around made the invasion of privacy even worse. When I had no money or optimism, just their presence would lighten my day. They made everything seem better and not nearly as devastating. It was different for Cynthia because she always had Noelle's unconditional love waiting at home for her.

One day I reached the point where I just said, *"fuck it!"* From then on, I made a conscious decision to *really* show it all. After the first five minutes of a scene, I would forget I was miked or even on camera. I allowed things to unfold naturally. If I was in a bad mood or Cynthia and I had an argument, that's what the crew had to deal with when they showed up. I gave the realness that people wanted to see. I wasn't down for faking the funk or living in a made-for-TV world. I'm that guy who has the balls to walk down the busiest street in Atlanta buck naked. So, getting in front of the cameras and letting it all hang out became nothing for me.

Cynthia's Lost & Found

I made it my business to review the previous seasons and familiarize myself with the women that would be sharing the next six months of my life. Kandi came off as easygoing, while drama seemed to follow NeNe, Sheree Whitfield and Kim Zolciak. I tried to keep a neutral mindset because I wanted to give everyone a fair chance. My first scene with the cast (except Kim) was the infamous Mother's Day brunch at my home. Thinking Kandi and I would have no problem connecting, I was surprised when I couldn't seem to get on the same page with her energy. She seemed guarded and standoffish.

I later learned it wasn't personal and that Kandi's aloofness is a part of her chill personality. Though we've yet to develop the depth of friendship she has with Phaedra, we grew to get along fine. That brunch actually turned out to be a memorable day for all of us. Our hen talk unleashed the controversy centered on Phaedra insisting she didn't know how far along she was in her pregnancy. By the end of the day, we were fuller from the buffet of inconsistencies than we were from the food.

My next scene with Phaedra featured us en route to the Steeplechase horse races. Peter, Dwight, Phaedra and I shared a limo to the race. Phaedra's was paying homage to Tammy Faye Bakker with a full face of theatrical makeup. Dwight looked like he was auditioning for the role of ringmaster for Ringling Bros. and Barnum & Bailey Circus.

Someone brought up the discussion of marriage and kids during our ride. The conversation prompted me to ask Phaedra if her pregnancy was the first child for her and Apollo. She responded with an unequivocal "yes" and proclaimed she could only be impregnated by a "clean man." I thought, *"She couldn't have meant what just came out of her mouth. This cannot be real."* I kept looking out the window thinking Ashton Kutcher was gonna pop out of a van with his own crew and tell me I had just been *Punk'd.* When Peter heard her comment, he didn't skip a beat in asking what Phaedra meant by it. Peter knew that Apollo had served time in prison and felt Phaedra's idea of a "clean man" was certainly unlike any definition he'd ever heard.

Phaedra came across as country-crazy and proud of it! I loved that she was unconventional in every possible way. Back in the day, I could imagine

Marriah

Mari

oin Us for the

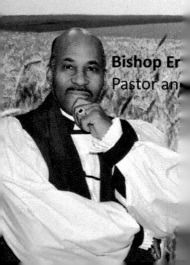

Mt. Carmel Chu

ME
CONFE
20

Bishop Er
Pastor an

her holding the title of Miss Watermelon Patch and Peach Preserves (four years in a row). Everything about her personified the South: her speech, clothes, jewelry, makeup – *and especially her mannerisms.* I was still new to Atlanta and had no frame of reference for her southern belle type. *If we have those in New York City, I'd never had the pleasure of meeting one.*

Getting acquainted with my fellow housewives called for the donning of my Miss Congeniality smile, gown and sash! Did I say sash? Sorry, I meant shield! Out the gate, Sheree and I didn't hit it off. I never felt totally relaxed in any setting we shared and was always confused by my interactions with her. She was so nice and sweet whenever we were together but would say hurtful things behind my back. We never got to know each other well, so it was disheartening that she was consistently negative and mean-spirited about me. When it was all said and done, she was just someone I worked with, and I chose not to take any of her actions personally.

Watching the first couple seasons of the show, you would think NeNe was the inspiration behind *Diary of a Mad Black Woman.* In our time together, I never saw her that way. She was just real and didn't have a problem speaking her mind. NeNe and Kim were actually friends when the show started. NeNe played a significant role in Kim's addition to the ensemble. As their friendship started to fall apart, NeNe and I began to bond. Kim and I always had an unspoken respect for one another until my closeness with NeNe became, in her eyes, a conflict. Once they severed ties, Kim pegged me as Team NeNe and killed any chance of us building a friendship.

In truth, I was just trying to get to know everyone. I refused to jump through pointless hurdles to prove myself worthy of anyone's friendship. Kim operated in a vacuum and never even visited my home. I went to hers *once,* under the pretense of a spa party – *if that's what you want to call it.* It was the episode where Kim ate pizza while lying under some type of red laser machine that was supposed to evaporate body fat. *Not really my idea of a spa treatment.* After leaving Kim's that day, I treated myself to a real spa visit. I didn't need to burn any fat, but I damn sure need to melt away the tension brought on by all the insanity.

Though NeNe was labeled the villain on the show, she and I were able to establish a loyalty that I could not achieve with the other ladies. She was my tenured professor at Reality TV University and I was determined to graduate at the top of her class. We talked like sisters and stayed on the phone all hours of the day. Our constant gabbing grew to irritate the hell out of Peter. He felt like every time I was on the phone, I was talking to her. He started to come off as controlling, and NeNe made it openly known that she was opposed to men who tried to control women.

NeNe and Peter eventually exchanged harsh words. Both being alpha personalities, it became a clash of two titans. Their disagreement resulted in a lapse of my and Peter's friendship with NeNe. Once again, I found myself in the middle of a battle that I'd not instigated. NeNe's position bothered me because there was no way in hell I'd ever allow anyone to control me, especially a man. It hurt knowing the three of us fell out over such a silly and trivial matter.

The notorious *friend contract* I gave NeNe is a perfect example of how a RHOA mosquito bite could turn into a bullet wound. Originally, I wrote the contract to clear the air after Peter and NeNe's argument. I was also battling stuff with some of the other girls. The aftermath of it all had me thinking, *"Damn, these women are such a trip, I need a friendship contract just to get along with them."* The other ladies knew NeNe was my girl and went out of their way to ridicule our alliance. The contract was clearly intended as a joke and attempt to lighten the mood. Unfortunately, in the world of reality TV, the more a misunderstanding is blown out of proportion, the better!

I thought the contract would be a no-brainer and a hilarious icebreaker. I envisioned giving it to NeNe and we'd both fall on the floor laughing, make up and the shit would be over. *The joke was on me!* I had enough egg on my face to sponsor a community Easter egg hunt. The women branded me as a crazy, fatal attraction that was in love with NeNe. Behind the scenes, I didn't know NeNe had been coaxed into circulating the letter, subsequently making me look like a *single black female*.

Social media criticism added a dreadful beating of its own. I realized I was in a big league game that I had no idea how to play. The drama became larger than life! It made me stand out in a dysfunctional way and was nothing close to the admiration I was used to receiving. It was disconcerting and also the first time I'd been in the company of women who put so much effort into being malicious for no reason.

Between Contract Gate, and her disagreement with Peter, NeNe and I didn't talk for weeks. The ordeal was the only disagreement we'd ever had on the show. We eventually talked and worked through the nonsense, and the whole fiasco was a turning point in our friendship. In the reality arena, one thing you don't want to be is forgettable. Putting that contract into NeNe's hands took care of that for me! Someone always has to carry the Crazy Flag, and that season it was me!

Peter's Coach Class

The *Real Housewives of Atlanta* put Cynthia in a circle of women who, under normal circumstances, would never have collided with her world. The only one she gravitated toward was NeNe. I've always felt they were so opposite, they became attracted to each other's differences. On the show, NeNe is known for saying she was "a stripper not a whore." I respect that NeNe did what she had to do as a single mother to feed her child. She had a hustle and a drive you couldn't help but bow down to. Initially, we bumped heads because we were both bullheaded, but we managed to get past our beef and grow closer. Cynthia and NeNe bonded over their differences, while NeNe and I clicked because of our similarities. She was even present when I proposed to Cynthia in April of 2010.

RHOA producers had a close watch on our plans to marry. They didn't hesitate to remind Cynthia and me that the show was called *The Real Housewives of Atlanta*. We made sure they understood our wedding plans were a top priority and the whole reason behind Cynthia's move to Atlanta. They couldn't wait to film Cynthia walking down the aisle!

While we allowed millions to watch our wedding, we've never allowed cameras in our bedroom. Producers have asked a thousand times and we give them a big, fat "NO" every single time! Some people think that because you're on a reality show you don't have morals or principles. We weren't willing to turn our asses inside out for the world to examine. There would be no bathtub or soft porn scenes with us. Cynthia and I vowed that our angle would always be to give swag, attitude, charisma and total truth.

The reality rumor mill is loaded with lies about the cast being fed lines by producers. It's a bunch of BS! When producers show up to shoot a scene, they leave with whatever is provided. Their job is to follow a storyline and take whatever they want from it. They may capture a mix of good and unscrupulous material but only choose to show the scandalous shit. What's shown in the final cut may not be someone's best self or what they would prefer people to see, but it's always what they said and did.

Bullshitting for the cameras always catches up with you anyway. A tabloid reporter, blogger or microphone pack will eventually expose you're living one reality and portraying another for television. Like the time viewers watched Phaedra speaking in tongues after the backlash from her infamous butt-dial. NeNe managed to get a copy of a message Phaedra had unintentionally recorded on someone's voice mail. Phaedra knew the language she used in her voice mail would not only disqualify her for Santa's Nice List, but it would also get her kicked out the church Christmas play.

Phaedra's backpedaling was one of the many situations that primed my wife on how to deal with the constant *Reality Gone Wild* mess. It didn't take long for Cynthia to morph from fashion model to model employee. Someone like NeNe is always going to say whatever the hell she wants, but Cynthia is more guarded. She tells me all the time that I put her in positions that require her to defend herself against my perspectives.

I make no apologies to her or anyone else, because I'm only interested in showing what I'm really about. If you ask me the deal, I always give real talk. No sugar. No cream. That's why I agreed to be a part of the show. People like that I speak my mind and confront shit head-on. I can back up anything I say or do — *on and off camera*. Life is not meant for everybody to get along all the time. Differences are a part of the undercurrent that makes the show successful.

I don't have to operate within any boundaries because I have never received a dime of compensation from Bravo. Cynthia's the one who gets paid to hold the peach in the show's opener. That's why it's called *The Real Housewives of Atlanta*, not *The Real Husbands of Atlanta Housewives*. We are simply on the show to make *charitable contributions* to the storyline of our spouses. I'm not saying I don't I benefit from the fruits of her labor, but when the check comes, it has Cynthia Bailey's name on it. Her money is her money. I don't count her eggs.

If ever I ask Cynthia for money, it's treated like a loan. It bothers the shit out of me because I know I'm the first man in her life to give her the confidence to build a career outside of modeling. I instilled the boldness in her to be a boss lady, own a business and achieve success beyond the runway. Unlike her, I have always worked for myself. She doesn't understand the general principles of running a businesses or being an owner-operator, so she learns from me.

As a model, you're chosen for jobs and paid a ton of money to do the work. Cynthia has mastered the practice of amassing money and storing it away like squirrels put back food for the winter. I ain't mad at her. I understand she comes from a world where you have to condition yourself to be that way because you never know when the next job or paycheck is coming.

Since starting The Bailey Agency, she's begun to understand what it means to be a business owner, but she still doesn't fully get the cold-blooded realities of true entrepreneurship. I'm a realist and a street cat who knows if you do nothing, *nothing happens*. She hordes money; I invest it. I have to create every dollar that comes through my fingers. I don't get shit dropped into my lap. It's a constant state of *rise and grind*.

I'm always willing to take calculated risks with the hopes of growing our money. If I lose, *which I have many times*, I always find a way to bounce back on the boulevard. My wife doesn't operate from the boulevard, she operates from the avenue. Action has to be forced out of her. While she holds on to things, I release them and move to the next opportunity. I see the shot glass as half full. She sees a tiny crack down the side of it, draining out all the whiskey.

A lot of Cynthia's hesitation with money stems from the $150K investment she lost in my Uptown project. On the other hand, she gained hundreds of thousands of dollars from joining the show and all the endorsement opportunities that came with it. She won't let go of the Uptown shit. But if it wasn't for Uptown, I probably would have moved to New York instead of her relocating to Atlanta. Had she not moved to Georgia, she would've never had the opportunity to become an Atlanta Housewife. That's the real-real! By my math, my wife has quadrupled the investment she put into Uptown, *and then some*. The fact that the money she lost is still a topic of discussion is beyond my comprehension. Again, if you do nothing, nothing happens. I made it happen for Cynthia Bailey.

Cynthia's Coach Class

My first season on RHOA is one I'd pay to have surgically removed from my memory. With absolutely no reality TV experience or insight from my fellow housewives, I dove in headfirst and gave *everything*. Peter and I were open and transparent to a fault! In no way am I implying that our current participation in the show is premeditated or practiced. But now, like every other reality personality, we have boundaries on what is shared and what is strictly off-limits. What people do see is authentic, uncensored Peter and Cynthia. No rehearsals. No scripts. Despite what you've heard or read, it really is reality TV.

The job doesn't come with *CliffsNotes* or a reference manual. Peter and I felt it would be less energy for us to be honest than to embellish. Our *mission of truth* did a lot of damage to us as individuals and as a couple. It was more draining than either of us anticipated, and the process was

like having a starring role in the movie, *Groundhog's Day*. We lived everything four to five times – in real life, when the episode aired, reruns and a
final blow during the reunion show. Trust me when I tell you that an old
wound is always one surface-scratch away from being reopened.

One of the toughest times in our first season was getting through the
episodes chronicling the money I put into Uptown. I made the substantial investment into Peter's new restaurant because my understanding was
always that it was a loan. I was devastated to learn I'd lost my money.
Grasping that it wasn't coming back was a little bit too much reality for
me. The money was a stash I'd put in savings and partially used to pay
our household expenditures. It was quite a nice chunk of money. I hadn't
realized how much I'd given Peter until most of it was gone. I was very
angry and wanted him to replace the money, but I knew he couldn't.
Watching the episodes about our finances quickly dug up what we had
already buried. We couldn't take a break from our own reality.

Back then, I hadn't built a fan following and people didn't know me.
There was no viewer sympathy or support for what I was experiencing.
The public scrutiny and backlash was unbearable. Viewers took to social
media and blogs ranting about how Peter was the wrong guy for me and
had swindled me out of my money. Others speculated he was beating me,
based merely on his choice of words and tone during our television arguments. Fans didn't hold back in telling me how stupid I was for accepting
Peter's proposal and that our marriage would never work. Some even felt I
should've stayed with Leon and married him. It was awful!

The nastiest story I read was concocted by some girl who claimed she'd
spent the night with Peter in an Atlanta hotel. I'm a super-secure woman
who never plays the role of fidelity warden in my relationships. Besides,
Peter is the type of man who can't get home fast enough at the end of the
night. Still, I was deeply bothered by the accuser's claims. Those closest to
us brought no relief by stirring the pot and asking me, "How can you be
sure Peter never went to the hotel with her? Where was he that night? How
do you know her story isn't true?"

It was annoying to watch people feed into the allegations. I knew it was all bullshit when this same female claimed that Peter had bought her an expensive handbag from Gucci. Truthfully, this part about the purse had me laughing so hard that pee was rolling down my leg. Let's be clear, I'm not saying my man didn't have a car and gas money to get to the mall, *but that was about it.* And I knew damn well he didn't have money to be buying Gucci anything – especially for some ol' skank. If any woman was getting something from Gucci – it was going to be my black ass.

For some women, seeking out attached and unavailable men is a sport. In our case, some were looking for bragging rights that they had been with Peter or could have been with him. It wasn't uncommon for women to show up at Uptown dressed to the nines, expecting to see Peter. It was all unfamiliar to me. I'd never had the mentality that if a man said hello or made eye contact that he was checking for me. A certain type of woman can be delusional in assuming a man is sweating her if he even looks in her direction.

Peter and I are both attractive people who are on national television – *every week*. With good reason, the show made us borderline paranoid about who we hung around or invited into our lives. Little Ms. Gucci Bag made Peter realize he had to be even more careful about the women he allowed in his environment. He also knew he had to walk that fine line between being friendly and being *extra* with random women. We would lay in bed at night in awe, wondering what we had gotten ourselves into. Deep down, we both knew my signature on the dotted line was a gateway to that kind of crap being our *new normal.*

Our starting season also paralleled the economy's blistering fall, and the show proved to be a lucrative gig during hard times. Though my salary wasn't the inflated figures plastered all over the Internet, the show was (and still is) a great way to make a living. Many of the salary assumptions listed on social media sites were laughable. One online source had Peter making $75,000 a season. The franchise is centered on the lives of the women. It's kind of an unspoken notion that when the wives bring money into their households, everyone under their roof financially benefits.

I'd love to see the husbands paid for the share of drama they infuse into the show. In our first season, Peter and I had family issues, money woes, got engaged and married. He was a major part of all my storylines. It would have been virtually impossible to capture my essence without including him. Since Peter's dominant addition to the franchise, I've noticed other husbands and partners have made anchoring contributions to their mate's narrative. I've always felt Peter had a lot to do with how pronounced spousal input has grown across the board. Peter even made *Atlanta Housewives'* history by being the first husband to sit on the couch during a reunion show.

Bravo has an amazing and generous platform for its cast that you can't find anywhere else. Drama, intrigue, battle of the wits and bickering are the products of great reality TV. Where else in the world can you earn a paycheck for arguing with someone who pissed you off or you already don't like? Just like Apple's profits come from the number of tablets and iPhones sold – RHOA's product is the housewives, and its returns hinge on our sensational disagreements. In the reality business, a Broke Drama Queen is an oxymoron.

If you have any type of entrepreneurial spirit, it's a perfect vehicle to spotlight your hustle. I was initially slow to act, but I know most people would leap at a chance to have such a public podium at their disposal. Commercials are very expensive, but what Bravo offers is better than a twenty-second spot! You and your business venture are actually featured on the show…in your own scene…and you get paid to do it! Former New York Housewife, Bethenny Frankel, is a great example of a housewife rags to riches story. *Forbes Magazine* reported that Bethenny sold her Skinnygirl adult beverage line to Jim Beam for a reported $100 million. How's that for turning your dreams into a *reality*?

Peter's Turbulences

At the end of our first season, I gave an interview to *UPTOWN Magazine* (no affiliation with my former restaurant). In the article I said I liked Kandi, but she got played by Kim. I couldn't stand Phaedra. Sheree thought she was cute, but wasn't. NeNe had a big-ass mouth, and Kim was crazy as fuck. Fans and critics viewed the article as a dig. I saw it as me giving honest answers to the questions I was asked. I went into the interview with no agenda other than to be truthful about the experience of my first season…and I was.

I didn't sign a contract relinquishing any rights to Bravo, and I controlled my own voice in the media. The release of my *UPTOWN* interview (and several others like it) proved that I had my own access to media outlets. In our second season, some of the women mentioned in that article came at me with guns cocked, blazing and ready to take me down. Ironically, the show's producers had started to see who I really was and wanted to capture a *more balanced* Peter in Season 4. They liked me, knew I was a good guy and wanted to flip the script a bit.

I was glad the laxer side of me was being unveiled. The previous season had people thinking they had the right to publicly say anything to me that popped in their heads. Like a run-in I had with a guy at Home Depot during our first season hiatus. I had just finished my purchase and was headed to the parking lot when the guy yelled from the back of the line, "Hey Peter, when you gon pay Cynthia back her damn money?" I blacked out. I went back in the store and told him, "Motherfucker, you can kiss my ass!" From the tone of my voice, he knew what it was gon be if he took his bullshit a step further. He checked himself quickly. I didn't want to hear that kind of noise anymore. I was done with folks thinking they knew me like a play cousin.

Cynthia, on the other hand, was obsessed with the blogs and stayed on them 24/7. NeNe would beg her not to read them, but she was sick over the fact that people saw her as NeNe's spineless sidekick. She didn't want to be known as the simple-minded, dense housewife. Even our family and friends were badgering her about how our characters were coming across, especially mine. Asinine social media comments had Cynthia giving second thoughts to me *and us.*

Cynthia dealt with the public ridicule by withdrawing. She became depressed and started to believe the hype. We would have massive arguments almost daily. She was never in the mood for loving and became completely turned off to any type of intimacy. The drama was killing our sex life. I went almost three months with absolutely no ass! It was hard for me to roll like that.

Every relationship has turmoil, but it was ruthless having ours play out two to four times a week in reruns and social media gossip. By the time a season airs, six to nine months have already passed. Regardless, there is something about seeing a situation for the first time on television that makes it feel brand new. Watching and reliving the struggles of our lives through a flat screen would interrupt our healing and sometimes bring back emotions that were stronger than the day of filming.

Whatever is wrong in a reality couple's relationship becomes intensified by the process. Where normal couples can squash a disagreement in one night, reality duos can take a year (or two) to get through it. Most end up in divorce court because the marriage isn't strong enough to endure constantly seeing, hearing and reading about every fuck up in the relationship. In our world, a manageable, stovetop grease fire can become an uncontrollable forest fire overnight. Even the strongest marriages struggle to survive.

There's no outlet to care for the cast off camera. It's an ice-cold setup, and if you're not dressed for the weather – YOU'RE FUCKED. I don't recommend it for fragile or psychologically weak couples. There should be therapists working behind the scenes to support the cast through all the problems and social media hostility. On another level, though, I get it! It's a business Bravo is running, not an elementary school. When you're hurt or emotionally injured you don't go to the infirmary – *you shoot the next scene.*

I know it's not about me, and I would be an ass to think anything but. I don't walk around thinking I'm some fucking actor or Hollywood dude. It's reality TV! The show is not intended to promote the spouses, their opinions or business ventures. The show is about housewives in Atlanta and all their squabbling, drama, baggage and everyday bullshit.

When it's all said and done, my true satisfaction as a man and husband comes from seeing Cynthia succeed. I take a great deal of pride in helping to create a new lane and income stream for her. I'm content knowing her position in life is elevated, and her financial gain is also mine. I would not hesitate to admit that the show provides an incredible platform to establish greatness. So, even in the moments where I'm weighed down, I know I have to keep it moving. I have a lot of people depending on me. If I slip, *their asses will go completely off the cliff.*

Sometimes I get tired from the load of my responsibilities, but I never think about stopping or quitting. The beautiful thing about being alive today is that it has absolutely nothing to do with yesterday. I love the fact that I have a chance to fix all the shit that happened twenty-four hours ago. I pray to God for a long life that will afford me the opportunity to give my kids all the things they've missed. My participation in the show is part of my strategy for making things happen and allowing my personal goals to manifest.

RHOA is a roaring fire that I don't want to extinguish before Cynthia and I use its flame to see our way to the other side. It's a unique opportunity in that no one ever tries to block whatever hustle you want to feature. Win, lose or draw – they shoot it and allow your ambitions to be shown. When I built and opened my newest restaurant, bar ONE, I was given several occasions to highlight it. As a result, around 60 percent of bar ONE's traffic is from people who watch us on television.

I talk to customers all the time who walk through the doors hoping to see me or Cynthia, *mostly me*. After three tough years and a social media lashing out of this world, it's refreshing to meet supportive, sympathetic fans. Some come just to congratulate me on bouncing back with another business venture. It's a blessing to have the support of people who don't even know you. They just want to see us win.

Some days, their encouragement is just what I need to hear to make it to the next juncture. My bold female admirers also show up with a determination to check me out in the flesh. Many like my aggressive, strong character and just come with the hopes of touching, squeezing or pressing their titties against me. They ain't shy about letting me know that they don't see my behavior as arrogant. They make it a point to tell me if Cynthia can't make it work, they'd love the company of a Mandingo like me.

Whatever that means!

I'm just sayin'.

Cynthia's Turbulences

By the kickoff of my second season (the show's fourth) I was getting ac-climated to the flow and felt equipped to tackle some of my mean-girl cohorts. Though I hadn't completely come out of my shell, the demands were becoming more manageable. I was jumping out as my own woman and promoting my newly opened modeling school, The Bailey Agency. It was a relief not to be the new girl on the block anymore.

After joining the cast of *Glee*, NeNe had gone to California and wasn't around as much. Her absence allowed our audience to see a different a side of me. Before joining the show, I'd been known as a trailblazer in the fashion arena. I was all too happy to press the reset button and show-case a fresh perspective of myself as an Atlanta Housewife. I went into my sophomore year decked out in a Teflon corset with steel backbone reinforcement. Especially after social media bandits had reduced me to nothing more than NeNe's spineless whipping girl.

Viewers weren't privileged to the backstory of how scenes were orches-trated. I filmed with whomever I was scheduled to be with on a given day.

It wasn't *The Cynthia Bailey Show*, and I didn't call the shots. NeNe was the starlet and fan favorite. We were usually paired off because she wasn't talking to the other girls as much. As a result, we were more often featured together than with any of our fellow housewives. Even with me being a newbie, most of our scenes made it past the editing room floor. The producers knew we had a lot of fun and they liked our chemistry. The fact that we were friends and NeNe was outrageously hilarious only added to the entertainment value. The bottom line was that NeNe was the veteran headliner, and producers wanted to make sure she was featured as much as possible.

I could never figure out how being a loyal friend was all of a sudden synonymous with being gutless. The adoration and respect between NeNe and I was quite mutual. She cared about and depended on me, just as much as I relied on her. Our friendship worked on and off camera. We knew we could work through any situation. We had a real bond that was often coerced or manufactured in reality TV. Ours wasn't the type of friendship that was built for the dramatic purpose of severing ties in a soap opera-style season finale.

The break during my first season's hiatus provided some much needed time to reenergize and prioritize. It prepared me for the pivotal occurrence of including Noelle in more of my storyline. It was an easy and logical decision for me. Noelle was the center of my world, and I couldn't show the true me if she wasn't included. I made it a point for her to mostly be in scenes that included her dad. I wanted there to be no question of how instrumental Leon was in her life. I was concerned about her presence making sense in the big-picture narrative of my life. I didn't find it acceptable to have Noelle sitting at the kitchen table doing homework or standing under me while I was gossiping or throwing back a bottle of wine. Still, once you put your kid on television, it's almost impossible to appease everyone's opinion on your mothering choices.

The attention brought on by the show was a major adjustment for her. In Atlanta, most celebrity children attended school with kids of other famous people, but I didn't buy into that concept. I never considered that the show would make us famous *or even recognizable for that matter.* I was wrong and blindsided by our popularity. When your child is the only one in the classroom whose parents are on television, it can be met with really unfavorable consequences.

Noelle started to get bullied. She was drowning between two extremes – those who loved her and had her back, and those who switched sides in the hallway when they saw her coming. I thought my strict instructions to never discuss the show at school would make her life easier. I didn't want her to feel it was a card she needed to play or that she was better than anybody else. I wasn't looking for her to get special treatment or privileges.

I did everything I could think of to eliminate the possibility of adolescent locker chatter in Noelle's school life. The big uh-oh moment was that I didn't anticipate parents and teachers who would be bold enough to interrogate her. "Did we have to audition? Was it fun being on TV?" The adults got caught up and began making her feel more uncomfortable than the kids. It all contributed to an environment where Noelle could not flourish. The situation became bigger than her and she hated going to school.

Having skipped a grade in primary school, Noelle was already a year younger than her classmates. Prior to attending school in Atlanta, her age had never been a problem in assimilating with other children. She was always a leader, very talented singer and drama student. In her new environment, I noticed that she wasn't adapting socially. Her grades were falling and she stopped eating. Although she wasn't big on having breakfast in the morning, she was naturally a healthy eater. By lunchtime she should have been starving, but her packed lunch was coming back home untouched.

Parents would rotate shifts to serve the kids during lunchtime. I was friendly with most of them and began receiving calls asking if Noelle was okay. A few shared that she didn't seem like herself, and was frequently sitting alone and not eating. As a mother, I knew the reports were serious red flags.

I had proudly placed Noelle in that school because it was touted as an exclusive, private institution. The year she enrolled, she was one of only twenty-five students selected from more than four-hundred hopefuls. In hindsight, I realized the way the school operated was far too militant for Noelle's learning style. I'm one for tough love, but not to the point where it breaks the spirit. The manner in which the kids were taught proved to be too great of a contrast against how Noelle was reared. We had raised her to believe she was strong, beautiful, amazing and could accomplish anything.

This was a child who had eaten at the table with A-list movie stars and grown up around icons that ran multi-million-dollar companies. At her young age, her exposure had been greater than many adults would experience in a lifetime. While at school, she was hearing that she "wasn't good enough for the play...couldn't do this...or wasn't at the level to do that." When in actuality, my daughter lived in a world where one phone call could have put her on Broadway and bypassed all the formalities.

Noelle was sinking into the walls, so Leon and I decided to explore homeschooling. It removed a lot of the distractions and anxieties that were stagnating her growth. I loved the sense of control, but very much disliked the lack of socialization and peer interaction. A small part of me was also thrilled to have more one-on-one, mother-daughter time. She was growing up too fast, and I looked forward to having our weekly mani-pedi breaks.

Unfortunately, I missed the memo that twelve year olds prefer to experience those luxuries with friends, *not their moms*. I couldn't continue to ignore the value and necessity of Noelle being around other kids. After six months of homeschooling, she was ready to return to regular school. We found a great new charter school that she loved. Only this time, the tables turned and Noelle was getting into trouble for being *too social*! We traded one extreme for another, but she started to thrive in her surroundings. I was ecstatic to see her make new friends! Her father and I agreed that a well-adjusted and content "B" student was a better deal than a depressed and unhappy "A" student.

By the time our second season kicked off, all the stresses of getting Noelle settled were behind me. Dealing with a fresh batch of housewives became my new hemorrhoid. My first meeting with Porsha was a taping at her grandfather's home. I thought she was pleasant, but young-minded in a lot of ways. At times, she didn't seem to be aware of what she was saying or the effect her words carried.

I loved that she would get so excited to be a part of a conversation that her mouth would often write a check that her butt couldn't cash. From my own experiences, I knew Porsha had a lot of learning to do to gain reality-TV traction. She was like a picnic in the park swarming with flies – *beautiful and thoughtful, but aggravating as hell.* In all fairness, Porsha turned out to be a harmless sweetheart and definitely the kind of girl I could have fun with *265 days a year.* (Or is it *365 days?*)

Then there was Hurricane Kenya. Losing Sheree in the previous season, and learning that Kim didn't want to be involved in the upcoming one, made us all anxious to find warm bodies. NeNe and I especially wanted things to hurry along, knowing that the longer it took to find replacements, the longer it would be before filming started. I'd heard that Kenya Moore, a former Miss USA, was being vetted as a possible addition. It isn't uncommon for producers to ask current housewives for recommendations on new blood. They didn't always know where to find women in Atlanta who could bring it – but they knew we did.

The only exposure I'd had to Kenya was attending the premiere of a movie that Boris starred in and she produced. I called him to get the scoop on her and satisfy my curiosity on whether she would be a good fit. I have an apparent vested interest in the show doing well. It's no secret that successful reality TV is about provocative, drama-infused storylines. Lack of harmony and mismatched chemistry is a heavenly formula.

Everybody knows a crazy, cussing, funny, sexy, quirky bitch is ideal housewife material. It's a gift to see someone come on the show and go to extraordinary lengths to beat out everyone else in being the craziest. I don't get too deep into whether I like or dislike someone. For me, it's always about what's best for the show. If it's good for *The Real Housewives of Atlanta*, it's great for me!

Boris had nothing but glowing things to say about Kenya. He suggested the two of us talk, and gave me her number. During my initial phone conversation with her, she was nothing less than normal and amazing. She definitely seemed like someone I wanted to put in the mix. I decided to throw her a bone by inviting her to a *JET* Beauty of the Week casting I held at The Bailey Agency. It was a scene I'd put together; producers had no input on the cast or judges. In fact, their interest in Kenya had waned and they weren't particularly excited for her to be there. As a totally random coincidence, Kenya was a former *JET* Beauty of the Week, but *JET* executives knew nothing of her coming until I told them.

The casting call was a nightmare! There were moments where Kenya was straight up channeling Evillene, the wicked witch from *The Wiz*. Instead of bringing security to The Bailey Agency, she should've bought a broom to fly back to wherever the hell she came from. It was ridiculous how disrespectful she was to some of the participants. At one point, she was even barking advice on how they should walk.

I was pissed off to the highest level of pisstivity! We exchanged words after the casting, and I hoped I would never see her again. Hardly! My invitation to Kenya ended up solidifying her position, and her lunatic-girl-next-door recital was enough to land the deal. It turned out that Kenya Moore was just the shot of tequila with a twirl (I mean twist) of lime that the show needed.

Seeing Kenya's inaugural performance at the *JET* casting taught me it takes all kinds to produce good reality TV. I think Kenya is a smart busi-nesswoman who knows exactly what she wants and isn't afraid to go get it.

It's all good, clean fun that I would not change for anything. No matter how contentious the cast interactions became or social media criticisms escalated, I always felt it would have been a fatal lapse in judgment to exit the show after my first season. When that initial episode depicting my face aired, the seal was already broken. I would forever be a part of Bravo's Housewife sorority. More importantly, people would always feel some entitlement to cross into my private space. If my life was going to be forever changed, I needed the number of zeros in my checking account to change too.

When my *Housewives* ride is over, I want people to see that even in my highest of highs and lowest of lows, I never compromised my dignity as a woman, mother or wife. I want people to know that I portrayed the real me and never felt the need to depict a character. Even if I wanted to, I don't know how to be anybody else. I'm not a southern belle, incessant drinker or bully. I'm not even an actress. And for those who are *still* wondering, *The Real Housewives of Atlanta* is not a scripted show, but it is my and Peter's reality.

CHAPTER V
Three-Hour Layover
Our Wedding

Cynthia's Descent

MARRIAGE HAD NEVER been on my bucket list, nor had I even seen the possibility in my distant future. I'd always felt solid in my independence and enjoyed my life as a solo act. When I uprooted Noelle and left New York, I knew I was seriously devoted to more than just a courtship with Peter. Before him, I'd focused my romantic search on finding Mr. Right, rather than trying to become someone's Mrs. Until Death Do Us Part. The two were mutually exclusive in my mind.

The title of *wife* never offered me a sense of security I didn't already have, but turning forty and raising a kid alone had definitely triggered a shift in my values. Taking that walk down the aisle began to sound like not such a bad idea. Peter saw marriage as the ultimate commitment between two people. In every place I was nontraditional he was surprisingly a traditionalist – marriage being no exception. It wouldn't have sufficed for me to have just been his woman; he wanted me to be his wife. I guess there's some merit to the theory that when a woman doesn't pressure a man about marriage, he innately pursues the matter even harder.

I'd always attributed my apathetic views on matrimony to the abuse I watched my mom suffer in her marriages. Her first, to my father, was just after he'd turned twenty. She was only seventeen and already pregnant with me. Growing up, she never dated or even hung around boys her age. Her unfortunate fate was that she ended up pregnant and having a shotgun wedding with the first man she had slept with. Birth control wasn't an option at her disposal, because she and her mother never had such "ungodly discussions." During 1966 in Alabama, when women got pregnant, they got married. As a result, by the age of eighteen, my mom found herself trapped in an unstable marriage with two babies eleven months apart.

My mother has always been a strikingly beautiful woman. In her heyday, she could've doubled for the character Diana Ross played in *Mahogany*. My dad was incredibly handsome, but he was insanely jealous and insecure. If ever he didn't know my mom's whereabouts, he would recklessly assume she was with another man. He used every control tactic possible to keep her checked – from compressing her self-esteem to verbally and sometimes physically abusing her.

I was too young to remember a lot of the unhealthy disharmony in their relationship. When I became of age, my mother started to share stories about my dad's physical episodes. She carefully detailed the mistreatment she had withstood and the cruel discipline he administered to me as a child. One particular story happened during my potty-training years. My daddy was old school and saw a training toilet as a waste of money. He had a wild hair to train me on a restaurant-size vegetable can that had exposed jagged edges. Never mind the fact that gangrene could have taken my behind to be with Jesus at three years old! Thank God my mom had the good sense to cut a hole in the can's plastic lid and place it on top of the metal to protect me. According to her, it took me a minute to master potty training, but it only took my brain a split second to know not to sit on that damn can. I was told the price of my refusal was a spanking from my foolish father.

As a mother myself, I know that women sometimes tolerate unjust things for the sake of keeping their households together. However, most won't allow those wrongs to affect the lives of their children. Sadly, my mom was too afraid to challenge my father's insensible authority. She had been raised to honor her husband's decisions and manage whatever burdens came along with raising children.

She was from the school of Divorce Ain't An Option. She didn't have many examples of healthy relationships or amicable conflict resolution. Her mother was reared to be a submissive wife, who in turn subconsciously raised her own daughters to stay in a marriage at all costs. It was a long line of suppressed teachings. It would compare it to Stevie Wonder and Helen Keller being professors at a school for the blind. *Everybody functioned in the dark!*

Women didn't welcome domestic violence, but it alone was not grounds for a divorce. In those days, abuse was more commonly tolerated in exchange for food on the table and a keeping a roof over one's head. While the door of my maternal grandmother's home was always open for my mom to retreat with us, it came with my grandmother's criticisms. She would somehow find a way to blame my mom for her inability to make her marriage work. As much as my mother detested my father's handling of us, she felt stuck.

My parents divorced by the time I turned four. Shortly afterwards, my dad remarried and had a child with his new wife. It all bothered the hell out of my mother. Her existence became a dejected cycle of working, complaining and struggling. Very much like Peter's father, she awoke each morning to a robotic existence that choked her motivation to create the future she wanted. It wasn't instilled in her that there could be more promise for her life, outside of domestic rituals.

The pressure of a failed marriage and raising two daughters had consumed her youth. She was unhappy, living with the awareness that she hadn't established her own independence or career. The heaviness of her discontentment was always apparent. It was a justifiable resentment that I wholeheartedly understood. It wasn't purposeful and I probably would have reacted the same way. Miserable people unknowingly do things as a way of insulating themselves from reality.

When I was ten, my mother began telling my sister Malorie and me more graphic stories about our father. We were naive to all the things that transpired in their marriage and loved him dearly. We looked forward to visiting him and riding in his fierce, shiny car. It was always clean and polished to perfection. To this day, a man's dirty car is a litmus test for me. *I wouldn't have gone on a date with Denzel Washington if he'd picked me up in a dirty car.* Well, not really! *Maybe the date would have started with a carwash and cocktails.* I believe my daddy's obsessive cleanliness is partly responsible for my fascination with a spotless car. It could also be the reason I readily agreed to go on the *carwash date* with Peter that day he picked me up from the airport.

For a long time after our parents divorced, Mal and I maintained consistent contact with our dad and his new wife. We saw them as flawless, but our glorification of either prompted more stories from our mother about our father's domestic mistreatment. She took a vested interest in showing us that neither of them was perfect. We would hear the particulars on how our stepmother relentlessly pursued our father until she "stole him." My dad had been my mom's first sexual encounter, but in contrast, our mom harped on how our stepmother was quite the opposite.

My mom resented her for initiating a relationship with my dad while he was still married. The closer my stepmother got to my sister and me, the deeper it dug under my mom's skin. Malorie and I were sitting pawns in their chess game. What we thought were acts of kindness by our stepmother, were actually strategic maneuvers against our mom.

Around the time I was thirteen, my mother married into her second impaired relationship. He was a man who seemed happiest in the company of a cocktail. He was controlling and far from perfect, but was a great provider. In fact, my stepfather was the first entrepreneur in my life, owing two or three stores and a few restaurants. People went as far to label us "rich" because we had several cars and the nicest house on the block.

Unlike her marriage to my dad, my mother was an adult when she entered into a union with my stepfather. She could not blame any of their problems on her naiveté or youth. Even though he had his own set of issues, he always managed to take care of his business and family. Their relationship only lasted four years, and my only brother, Thomas, was the blessing that came out of it.

At seventeen, I started what eventually would amount to only a semester of college. Instead of having a two-hour commute driving from mom's, I moved in with my dad since he was only ten minutes from campus. Staying in his home was the first time I noticed a stark change in my stepmom's behavior toward me. She was petty, and mandated that I maintain my own separate supply of groceries and toiletries from the rest of the household, while she hoarded a stash of cakes, snacks and sodas under lock and key in her bedroom.

My social life was bound by a ten o'clock curfew. If I missed the cutoff, an inside mounted chain lock would override my house key. I saw that chain as a watchdog that alerted my stepmother of my arrival, forcing her to wake and grant me access into the house. My dad knew of her control tactics, but he never acknowledged or opposed them. I believe he initially tried to stand up to her, but she always won. It didn't take long to figure out she wore the Levi 501's in their family. It would have been a losing battle for me to challenge her authority. Her treatment of me infuriated my mother.

After living several months under my stepmother's rule, I'd had all I could take. I moved nearby into my boyfriend's place, whose name also happened to be Thomas. We were best friends and very much in love. He was nineteen and the first of many things for me. First boyfriend, first real relationship and the first man to tell me I was the most beautiful girl in the world. As crazy as it sounded, I believed him. It was an accolade I had never gotten from my father. Though I trusted and adored Thomas, our relationship became more of a brotherly-sisterly connection. He encouraged me to go north and pursue my dreams in modeling. He had a good intuition about where my life was headed. Just before my twentieth birthday, I was scouted by Wilhelmina Models and moved to New York.

Through the years, the relationship with my father remained a tense one, but I did all the right things expected of a *good* daughter. Even though he didn't deserve it, I was diligent in sending birthday gifts, Father's Day cards and little cheap box sets of cologne for Christmas. By his own doing, my father managed to live up to the disparaging image my mom had painted of him. I took solace in knowing that her hype of his bad behavior ultimately had no bearing on how I saw him. My outlook of my father was purely derived from my own interaction (or lack of) with him.

In our early thirties, my father called and asked to meet with Malorie and me. He wanted to share his side of what had gone down in his marriage to our mother. The mere request from him annoyed my mom. She couldn't imagine what explanation he had to offer after all the years that had passed. Mal was mildly interested but mostly indifferent. I was eager to hear his side. His divorce from our mother and subsequent marriage had placed a serious strain between the three of us. Once Mal and I became adults, the tension in our relationship snapped like a rubber band. I desperately needed the closure.

My father opened his sit-down by sharing there had been some recent issues in his marriage. The effects had left him vulnerable and at odds with our stepmother. Looking back, I think he led with the sob story to garner sympathy from my sister and me. I felt badly that the woman he had so boldly put on a pedestal had fallen from grace and broken his heart. Still, a part of me was screaming on the inside, *"Aha! Karma! That's what yo ass gets!"*

He was taking a slurp from the spoon of medicine he had dished out to my mother for so many years. My stepmother had wronged my father in a way that would have never occurred to my mom. It was astonishing to watch the same man who had stolen my mother's confidence to leave him, be emasculated by the very woman he cheated with.

The problems in his second marriage seemed to soften him, and he admitted to making some really poor choices in his relationship with my mother. Some of his marriage war stories supported our mother's versions. However, most of his accounts contradicted hers and leaned in his favor. He went on to apologize for the times he was checked out during our rearing, as well as his lack of financial support. He was regretful that he had only paid the very bare minimum in child support and cut it off the day we turned eighteen.

In the end, Mal and I accepted his apology. The three of us made a pact to be a family again and spend more time together. My mother was appalled by the truce, but happier than a pig in shit to learn his world had been shattered by his wife. Months later, my father patched up his issues with my stepmother and things went right back to the way they had been before. Unsurprisingly, my father failed to reciprocate Malorie's and my efforts to rebuild our broken relationship.

In a funny way, my dad is responsible for my professional success, because I was determined that I wouldn't end up with a man like him. He was a big part of why I never respected any marriage around me. As an adult, I loved being in committed relationships, but my true focus was always on creating a life opposite my parents' life. *I wanted choices.*

I didn't want to lay in bed at night next to a jerk that drained the worth out of me during the day. I feared ending up in a relationship that would smother my happiness, force me to become a mother before I was ready or marry the first man I laid down with. My backseat view of seeing my mother and aunts with mates who didn't appreciate them, conditioned me to run like hell from marriage. *Though I found getting engaged to be quite fun.*

Peter's Descent

I like the concept of two people getting together who are completely in love and devoted to one another. I have never been afraid of marriage, as long as it was with the right woman. My first marriage happened in my early twenties to a girl I'd known since the tenth grade. We weren't high school sweethearts, but we attended the same school. I knew she was a loner and really serious about her books. She was a pretty girl who appeared innocent and sweet. The boyfriend type, who wanted to lock a guy down; making her by no means…my type! I've always been a gentle hunter, who allowed the young lambs to get away. High school was no different. I never wanted the challenge of a steady girlfriend. My only focus was on wiling out and hanging with girls who were giving it up.

I went away to college after graduation and came back home during the Christmas holiday of my freshman year. I got a job at Abraham & Straus department store in downtown Brooklyn. While working one day, I looked up and saw the same bookworm girl from high school. At first, she tried to walk past and give me one of those, *that's the asshole from high school* looks. I managed to hem her up before she could sneak by.

I was surprised that we had enough in common to hold a twenty-minute conversation. It was the first time we had ever spoken or been that close. She was even prettier than what I'd seen from a distance: about 5'6", fair skin, curly hair, big brown eyes and freckles scattered over her face. *Maybe she was my type.* It was just like me to flip some shit that was a definite "NO" into an absolute "YES." I was about to mack down this exception to my "Don't Pet the Lambs" rule.

I really didn't know much about her, other than the fact that she had a royal asshole for a brother. I only knew him because we were in the same grade. He always missed school, and on the days he came, he was drunk or smoked out. We were living in very racial times where people overlooked shit strictly based on skin color. Both of her brothers had very fair complexions, curly hair and light eyes. They were on some DeBarge-look-alike shit. She was definitely a beautiful girl who resembled them, but her head was on right. Coming off the twisted racism of the '60s, a dark-skinned brother like me (as my wife would say) was not "in fashion." In those days in Brooklyn, you were fucked if you were one shade darker than Michael Jackson (the "Off the Wall" Mike).

I asked if she was available to go out with me that weekend, and she accepted without hesitation. My intuition was spot-on! She *was* one of those girls who wanted to lock a brutha down. She never uttered the words, but everything about her screamed it. We saw each other every day before I went back to school that January. I attended college in Tulsa, Oklahoma, and she was studying in Brooklyn. When it was time for me to head back to Oklahoma, she dropped out of school and moved there with me. She was really feeling me!

My true high school sweetheart was Chinese and Trinidadian. Her parents wanted her as far away as possible from my black ass. They had shipped her off to Edwards Air Force Base in Bakersfield, California. I had only moved to Oklahoma to be closer to her, but I no longer needed the hassle of the situation since my new girl was living with me.

When my soon-to-be wife made the move to Oklahoma, nobody threw her a parade. Her parents were separated and she was being raised by her grandparents. Her grandfather pastored a church in New York and they all lived in a tiny apartment above it. He wasn't exactly warm and fuzzy over the idea that his granddaughter was sinning with a boy she'd known for only a few months. After a year in the Midwest, everyone was happy to see us move back to Brooklyn. The '80s in Oklahoma was like living in Alabama in the '20s. Being called "nigger" twenty times a day got old, real quick! I was over the bigotry, and being home gave me a sense of peace.

New York City infused me with mad confidence. Just being back there was enough to give me the balls to marry my girl. It was a terrifying move, but I figured it was the right thing to do after the display of love she had shown in leaving her family to be with me in Oklahoma. I'd been taught that the cycle of life for a man was to get an education, marry a woman you cared about, have kids, go to work every fucking day and make a life for your family. That's what I was prepared to do.

We had a small church wedding with about fifty people. The reception was at the Ozone Layer, one of the hangout dives I frequented in Brooklyn. In our first year of marriage, we rented an apartment two blocks from my parents' home in Flatbush. My wife gave birth to our first child on August 3, 1983 – a daughter we named Porsche Alexandria.

I wanted everything life had to offer, so I transferred to city college in Brooklyn and continued my studies at night school. Blacks in New York with college experience were treated a little better than ones without it, *even if you didn't have a degree.* I landed a job with the City of New York. It freaked me out when I realized that my office sat directly across from the Abraham & Straus store where my wife and I had our first conversation.

I started off as a temporary employee, but my boss wouldn't let up until he got me a permanent position as a social worker. My first assignment was managing a caseload of over 300 people. I was twenty-three years old and sharing a work area with four other case managers in their forties. Our five desks sat side-by-side, aligned in a row like some elementary schoolhouse shit.

My peers seemed to dig me, but they couldn't understand how I had gotten their same job at my young age. Most of them had held their positions for twenty years *or more.* My white, female colleagues had been sitting in the same office chairs for so long that when they got up their asses held the form of the seat. All day long I stared at fucking family portraits, fake flowers, stacks of files and a shitload of paperwork.

It didn't take long for me to start thinking there had to be a better hustle out there for me. I only hung onto the job for its benefits. My wife had sickle-cell anemia and got really sick in the last four months of her pregnancy. When she was hospitalized, my health insurance covered all her medical expenses. It was one of the only perks about the job that forced me to get up every morning and keep punching the clock.

The position was also the first time I'd worked in an environment with gay men. Both my supervisor and a coworker (whose desk was right next to mine) were gay. I was fascinated by them. I couldn't believe there was such a thing as a man who really didn't like pussy! I wanted to know how they got to be that way. My curiosity, and our mutual love of music, helped us bond. They always had hot tracks playing on their desk radios and we used music to get through the struggles of the ratched workday. We grew to be close friends. *No HOMO, though!*

After two and half years of the off the chain caseloads, I was done! I couldn't see myself doing that shitty job for another eighteen years. Initially, I was amped about the opportunity because I thought I could help people better their situations. The city offered unbelievable incentives to folks on government aid, and paid for any program or schooling they wanted. Instead of using the opportunity to improve their quality of life, most people were hustling the system like scavengers.

This one particular family (the Festers), was the straw that broke my back. They were generational welfare hustlers. The grandmother had been on assistance for thirty years. These trifling-ass hoodrats were over 90 percent of my caseload. It was the type of leaching and ignorance that made me sick to my stomach. One day, I went to punch the time clock, and it hit me…*I wasn't changing their lives and they weren't changing mine.* The job had become like a jail, and I needed to get the hell out! I ripped up my time card, threw it on the floor and headed straight to JFK Airport on a one-way flight to Miami.

When I landed, I hit a newsstand and picked up a *Miami Herald* before calling my wife. I went straight to the classified section, saw a job listing for a Wendy's manager trainee program and took a cab to apply for the position. Back in New York, my wife worked as a restaurant manager at Wendy's. When I picked her up at the end of her shift, I would sometimes wait in the restaurant lobby and watch her do her thing. I saw all the nuances involved in managing the restaurant and a large team. I knew I could do the job too. Before working as a social worker, I'd held jobs at Dunkin' Donuts, Sizzler Steak House and KFC, so it wasn't a stretch to say I knew my way around hot grease. I was hired on the spot to begin training as a store manager.

Three hours after getting to Miami, I made the dreaded call to my wife. I phoned her on one of those huge cell phones that was big enough to beat the shit out of somebody. She had already been calling my desk all day and suspected something fishy was going on. I tried to talk fast and explain to her that I couldn't stomach my job another day. I told her the thought of paying our landlord $750 a month in rent for the next twenty years (like my father) made me want to vomit.

She asked how I expected her to pay the bills and take care of our daughter in my absence. I told her I had already found a job in Miami, and she could depend on me to make sure our expenses were covered. I wanted her to know I had everything under control, and I didn't want her to be pissed that I had just taken off. After I said the part about finding a job in Miami, the phone immediately went dead. I remember yelling into the phone, "Hello? Baby? You still there?" Either she'd hung up on me or that big-ass dinosaur phone dropped the call. I never did figure out which happened.

Six months later, my wife and Porsche joined me in Miami. In 1984, racial intolerance was lifting, but an infestation of Uncle Toms was on the rise. I had the pleasure of working for one who had a spit-shine, gold grill. He was my district manager, and he did everything humanly possible to try to convince me that being a Wendy's manager was the best fucking job in the world. On a weekly basis, he'd feed me dump trucks of bullshit on how I could have my own district in less than eight years. He was crazy as hell!

I had just left some Uncle Tom shit in New York. Why would I want to get back on the same plantation working with a different commodity? I always give him props though, because he taught me a lot of great business practices. I just had no ambitions of managing a damn region of Wendy's. I wanted to own them! The owner and founder of the Wendy's restaurant concept was a guy named Dave Thomas; mine was Peter Thomas. So, I took my ass back to Brooklyn to see where my famous surname could take me.

My dad got me a job as a day laborer on a construction site. In 1985, I was making $32 an hour, but I hated working in the extremes of 20° below and 120° weather. Quitting my construction gig forced me to enter into work that I wasn't proud of. Not having an income was never an option for me, and street hustling was the easiest way of keeping my family afloat.

By the time Peter Anthony Jr. was born in April 1987, I was the man – driving fancy cars and hanging with mobs of beautiful women. I was living between New York and Miami, where my street endeavors helped me prosper even more. I was going through the revolving doors of a treacherous world where I risked my freedom on a daily basis. Thieving cops were known to rob dealers and send them straight upstate to do hard time. Or even worse, I could have been robbed and killed by a street thug.

I took some of the money I had put back and opened a shoe store. Once I got it going, I sent for my family to join me. Truth be told, it was over between my wife and I before Peter Jr. was born. We had been together for six years and grew further apart each year. We rushed into marriage in our early twenties without really knowing each other. Once we discovered who the other was, neither was interested. We separated when Peter Jr. was around nine months old. We lived detached lives in different cities for years, but stayed legally married for another decade.

With all that happened in my first marriage, I was still open to the possibility of settling down and being with one woman. Meeting Cynthia twenty years after my first committed relationship, my heart told me she was the woman I had been waiting for. I liked that she saw me as an equal partner. She had a Plymouth Rock belief in me, and she backed it up with her actions by moving to Georgia.

We talked about creating a world of our own where she could jump on a plane at a moment's notice, model all over the globe and have an enviable life. We believed we could have an incredible existence together – with our beautiful supper club (Uptown) being a big part of it. But the recession had a plan to take us out like Hurricane Katrina.

In trying to keep Uptown going, everything that could go wrong, went wrong. The only bright spot in the darkness was an act of goodness by my landlord. He knew my history as a businessperson and offered to carry my rent for five months. He was a decent guy who would have held me down for another year if I'd needed him to, but it would have only put me deeper in the hole. The rent was just one aspect of my obligations. I was also struggling to pay utilities, vendors and employees.

Not being able to meet payroll was a cancer of its own. When you can't pay people, they take on a vicious sense of entitlement and start stealing from every end. I was desperate and delusional to think it was just a rut that would pass. The recession had shit upside down and people had literally stopped spending.

Everything in my life went south. My dad's retirement money and the last of my savings were tied up in my fading dream of Uptown. I could barely keep the lights on. Paying for a wedding seemed like a pie in the sky fantasy that would never happen. I became the poster child for angry black men. I was pissed off almost every day, and it was hard to feel anything else.

Watching my finances spiral out of control was like watching a movie about someone else's life. I loved Cynthia so much, and I still wanted to make her my wife. I had always thought marriage should never be about money, but I knew she'd already turned down three suitors that were easily $100-million men. I couldn't let her story end in financial ruin just because she chose love over money. I refused to let her get away! It was up to me to figure out how to throw a supermodel's wedding on a budget.

Cynthia's Control Tower

I always tried to flip negatives in my life into positives. Peter and I had begun to establish a home and life in Atlanta. There was no reason for us not to become man and wife. Noelle had also been questioning if Peter and I were going to get married. She was at an age where my choices would eventually flavor the ones she made as an adult. I didn't want to irresponsibly influence her principles in life. She had a way of making me look at things through a different lens.

I was also conscientious of the fact that people in Georgia were especially comfortable with interviewing complete strangers about their marital status. I had begun to feel the heat from the flames of hell that came with shacking up in the heart of the Bible Belt. Two years in, Peter made his intentions official by asking for my hand in marriage. It was time to plan a wedding!

Since I never had any ambitions of marrying, I certainly had none for a big, lavish wedding. I envisioned Peter and I getting hitched somewhere on a private beach (maybe Anguilla) surrounded by a handful of friends and family. A wedding wasn't the only thing I hadn't foreseen in my future – *our reality show was the other hiccup*. Being on television weekly meant we had a mini nation of people who were expecting invitations. My vision of a quaint wedding was dead before I ever birthed it.

Peter has great architectural taste and knew a venue off the beaten path would be right up my alley. Earlier that year, he had attended an event at Atlanta's renowned Fernbank Museum of Natural History. He thought the site would be perfect for our wedding and reception. I got chills the first time he took me there. When I stood in its thirty-foot-ceiling atrium, surrounded by the life-sized dinosaurs, I knew I had to get married under the belly of one.

Against my every attempt not to, I turned out to be a typical bride, with my wedding plans focused on everyone *but me*. The only element

I managed to stand firm on was that I wasn't wearing a white dress. I was initially sold on wearing a black gown, but I wanted to make a bold fashion statement, so I opted for a hue in the platinum family. My BFF and acclaimed celebrity stylist, Kithe Brewster, was the inspiration behind my dress.

For most brides, the dress is the piece de resistance of the wedding, *but it wasn't for me.* I just wanted to look good. I gave Kithe total control over the design, as long as the end product was truly Cynthia-inspired. He came up with the impeccable couture creation and Rubin Singer designed the dress. I didn't see the final rendition until a week before the wedding, and with the exception of a few minor adjustments, it was flawlessly me.

When Peter and I started planning our wedding, we had a significant amount of money spread over multiple accounts. By the time we reached the midway point, we were basically working with pocket change that could be managed in a piggy bank. Thank God for Tony Conway of A Legendary Event! He took being a guardian angel to a whole 'nother level. After sitting down with him, we refused to consider other caterers. He was accommodating and wanted to give us the wedding he thought we deserved – *regardless of our finances.* He insisted we not worry about the cost, even if it took us twenty years to pay him back.

Tony's focus was entirely on making our wedding impeccable. He was dedicated beyond comprehension, and I will forever be indebted to him! We became friends as a result of his generosity and ability to turn a stressful situation into a *legendary event.* Peter would be my new husband, but Tony was the knight in shining armor that made our wedding spectacular. Even today, we won't do an event without Tony and his extraordinary team. Thankfully, we can now pay him without postdating the check.

Under the financial weight of Uptown's decline, Peter was also juggling the responsibilities of supporting our household, paying business expenditures and managing our wedding costs. My mother and sister could see we were in trouble and continually questioned whether marriage was an appropriate next step. People would be surprised to learn that my family genuinely loves Peter. Prior to our marriage, their only reservation was that Peter's financial issues were becoming mine.

I'd always been able to more than adequately support myself, and my family had only seen me live an extravagant lifestyle. When I went virtually bankrupt, they felt like they did too. There was no one else to resolve money matters or pick up the slack. I was the community bank, and when my funds evaporated the neighborhood reserve dried up too. It naturally made everyone leery of my union with Peter.

My folks were conservative and old-fashioned. Peter was a hustler and risk-taker who (in their eyes) represented uncertainty. I think it's instinctive for a parent to worry about its child. Even though I was a forty-year-old woman, I was still my mother's baby. As long as Peter's finances were shaky, she couldn't get comfortable with the thought of us being married. It was hard for her to understand that I was completely sold on his vision.

You can always find money, but you can't always find love. That's why I contributed all I had to give Uptown the best shot at succeeding. It was a huge part of our lives and had become one of the characters in our storyline. We shot a lot of key and memorable scenes there. We felt compelled to keep it going and didn't want to lose it in front of the world. We truly did everything in our power to hold on, but it reached a point where we had to jump ship or go under with it.

We never anticipated how devastating or lasting the recession would be. It had a profound effect on our relationship, finances and intimacy. We thought Uptown would be our retirement nest egg. I, for one, never expected it to fail and certainly didn't intend to lose my life savings. What started off as a $15,000 contribution, became another $25,000…then another…and another…until I lost track. Once I'd given Peter the first hundred thousand dollars, I felt the only way I could protect my initial investment was to continue fronting him capital. I kept thinking every round would be the one that would get us back in the black. I was wrong.

My series of uncharacteristic money decisions had my mother and sister reflecting on the men who had pursued my hand in marriage. *Each could have set me up for life.* Why had I chosen to take roots with one who had serious money troubles? The reason was clear and simple in my mind. I saw Peter as a boss and a visionary. Donald Trump had lost millions, went bankrupt more than once and managed to come back. Why couldn't Peter? I believed in him with my whole heart and wanted to keep the lights on in the eyes of the man I loved.

Weeks before the wedding, everything came to a head. We were so broke we didn't have money to cover our alcohol bill. Since my father had done so little for me throughout my life, my mother suggested I ask him for help. I was more interested in soliciting his support just to see if he would rise to the occasion. I called and gave him the *"what had happened was"* version of my and Peter's situation. I asked for $5,000 but told him I could make $3,000 stretch to take care of everything.

Even though I promised to pay him back as quickly as possible, part of me hoped he would give it to me as a back-pay, child support gift. My heart longed to hear him say, *"Baby, you don't have to pay me back. I want to do this for you! I owe it to you!"* Sadly, those words never reached my ears, and my heart felt like it had been sliced by one of those *As Seen on TV* Ginsu knives. He immediately started in with a variety pack of excuses, "Well, there's a lot going on in our household. We just paid the down payment for our cruise. I wish you would have asked earlier..." He didn't even have the courage or respect to just give me a straight up "NO."

I didn't know the specifics of my father's finances, but I knew he did well for himself and could have made it happen for me if he wanted to. It was the only time in my life that I needed him to come through for me and he devastated me in every way. It hurt me to my core. I had already asked him to walk me down the aisle and his conscious decision not to give me the money didn't change my mind. Revoking the invitation wouldn't have gotten me the money anyway.

Our wedding was set to be RHOA's Season 3 finale, and I was too stressed to be thrown off course by his selfishness. My mother agreed to loan Peter and I the $3,000. The person who had been my rock over the years was also the one who saved my wedding day.

One daddy don't stop no show!

Peter's Control Tower

When you're from the streets and your brain gets the signal that your life is slipping, it automatically goes into survival mode. Cynthia and I began planning our wedding when life was prosperous, with money to spare. The participation in our reality show also put us in a position to do mutually benefiting barters with local businesses. I would take business profits from here and there to do creative, *legal* investments. Extending short-term, hard money loans (with 25 percent interest tacked on) was profitable with quick turnarounds. When our paper got tight, even that option faded to black.

Our circumstances turned dire and the likelihood of having our dream wedding (or any wedding at all) started to look grim. My hood sensibilities came up with an idea to get help from our production company. I called them up and told them our ceremony was in jeopardy if we couldn't come up with the cash to pay our remaining expenses. I drilled home the point that if we didn't get their backing, there would be no wedding. No wedding equaled no grand Season 3 finale! They finally agreed to give me the money, only problem was, *I put the check into Uptown's account...* hoping I could flip it.

I thought I had enough time to double or at least replace it, but the recession had a vice grip on people's spending. Every day was worse than the one before. Weekends were mega-earning days for Uptown, but the economy had reached a point where our Friday and Saturday volume wasn't much better than a Monday or Tuesday, which were our slowest days. I couldn't recoup the money fast enough, and the production company panicked when they learned I'd misused it. Cynthia knew nothing of my proposition or that I had even received money from them, until they ratted me out!

The day they went behind my back and told her about the advance, was the same day I was able to replace it. That morning, I called my boy Kedar Massenburg and asked for help. He was the former president of Motown Records and founder of Neo Soul music. I explained to him that I was in a corner and needed him to spot me some cash until I could get back on my feet. He wired me $15,000 within a matter of hours. I took the funds straight to our caterer, but by the time I got home the producers had already dropped the bomb on Cynthia. I told her that I only did it because I didn't want to let her down, but she was still fuming. We wound up having a heated argument and it all went down on camera. When we were done, I threw the whole fucking crew out of our house.

It takes very little for Cynthia to go into level-ten panic mode. She was used to earning $10,000 a day on a single modeling job. She never left money on the table. I liked that she took pride in building new relationships – even with small, emerging clients. If they were willing to make her the face of a campaign, she would spend $500 on a plane ticket to go do a $1,000 job. Her mindset was that she still came home with more than she left with. She was good with managing money and very conscientious. She couldn't relate to me blowing thousands of dollars every time it touched my hands.

No one can ever convince me that the producers weren't fantasizing that my engagement to Cynthia would be her fourth broken one. They hinted that we might even want to consider postponing our marriage until the following year. At one point, they had the balls to tell me to my face that "it may not be a good time for us to go through with the wedding." I wouldn't have put it past them to be secretly hoping that the next season would open with her dating some recognizable millionaire who could boost ratings.

The move would've been a crapshoot for me, but remarkable television for them. They weren't banking on Cynthia *not* being a materialistic woman. She managed to work through her anger, forgive me and continue planning our wedding. They must have bumped their heads and forgot we were on reality TV, not a scripted soap opera. They can't just kill Peter Thomas off like a Telenovela villain. I thought they knew!

Cynthia's Runway

The day of our wedding, I awoke anxious for it to be over and done. My tank was on E and I had nothing left. There was a camera in my face from the time I opened my eyes at 8:00 a.m. that morning until 1:00 a.m. the next day. Other than champagne, I went the whole day with hardly any other beverage, and I barely remember eating at the reception or even tasting our wedding cake. The mental fatigue I'd endured in the planning process was much worse than the physical. *I was completely exhausted.*

My glam squad and I spent most of the day shooting in my bridal suite. They primped, plucked, bustled and fussed over every inch of me. It was a mechanical day that felt more like one of my catalog shoots, rather than the high of my wedding day. There was so much happening, I was delirious. I just wanted to get through another hair and makeup session, meet Peter at the end of the aisle and sleep in for the next three days.

The wedding could not start until the entire cast of *Housewives* was present and seated. The women were always notoriously late, and the delays left me drinking even more champagne. The dead time also gave our guests an opportunity to get good and saucy, which was a homemade recipe for infinite drama.

Speaking of which, little did I know my mom and Malorie were elsewhere in the venue nestling their necks in a noose. They were still distressed over the fact that I was financially and emotionally in a place they had never witnessed. They were doubtful of Peter's ability to support a family and viewed him as moody and stressed out.

He had a serious chip on his shoulder and didn't give a damn about what anybody else thought. His irritability created arguments and tension between the three of them. My mom and sister felt they were protecting me by entertaining a plan to foil the wedding and allowing our marriage certificate to conveniently disappear. Luckily, their better judgment prevented them from carrying out the absurd idea.

Hours after the ceremony should have started, I was given the nod that it was finally time. In that moment, it hit me that I was really getting married. I was so focused on planning the wedding that I had not taken the time to relish in the sacredness of the moment. The weeks leading up to the day had been dreadful, but in the ninth hour we were able to make everything materialize. A typical bride's thoughts should be filled with visions of slipping her hand through her father's arm and taking in all the smiling faces of her friends and family. Instead, mine were drunk with relief that it was the last day of filming and Season 3 would be behind me.

As I began my descent toward Peter, I began processing all the irony that had overwhelmed the day, particularly, the situation with my father. He had done absolutely nothing to make the day possible, but was escorting me down the aisle. Funny, he was all too happy to share our spotlight. Looking back, it really wasn't that funny at all, knowing that my wedding day was the last time I saw or spoke to him.

There was no spark of emotion in my body until I saw Peter tearing up at the end the aisle. I knew in my heart we were both feeling that in spite of everything, we were living a moment that made all the obstacles worthwhile. We shared tears of happiness. Peter knew a woman was walking toward him who had sacrificed everything she had to be with him. Life is about choices, and mine was to stand next to him and become Mrs. Peter Thomas. I had not a single regret.

Peter's Runway

Cynthia had gotten past the humiliation of what I'd done in my desperation to cover our final wedding expenses. The last-minute predicament was finding money to pay for the alcohol. She asked her dad to spot the tab, he refused and it crushed her. Whatever leftover hope there had been for their reconciliation was buried in her disappointment. It wasn't about the money for Cynthia. It had more to do with a woman's belief that she should be able to financially count on her father for something as important as her wedding. Especially, a father who had failed to provide support beyond a chicken shit, court-mandated order. When her father told her he wasn't in a position to give any money – in Cynthia's mind – *it was a wrap.*

The day of our wedding was a spiritual high for me. I kicked it off by meeting my boys and picking up my tuxedo from the suit-maker. The CEOs of *UPTOWN Magazine* and *Vibe* magazine were my best men. They were beating my balls the whole time and tripping over how I had managed to make it all come together in the final days. We had a bottle of Cîroc vodka, and I think we drank the whole damn thing in the course of our smack talking. We were so bombed; I don't even remember the drive to the wedding site.

Walking into the ceremony, the first two people I saw were my mom and dad. I wondered if I had invited them to sit in the front row and witness the biggest fucking disaster of my life. Looking at them sobered me. I felt nothing short of terror and everything around me became a blur.

The guests arrived like spectators filling an arena to see if the bout of the heavyweights would happen. I didn't know 95 percent of the people present. I felt like I was getting married in a room of practical strangers, most just there to see if the day would crash and burn. Would I get knocked out in a first round TKO or would Cynthia be a front-page, runaway bride?

The Cîroc had started messing with my head, and I was replaying all the engagement rings that Cynthia had given back. She told Russell Simmons "no" and he had $300 million in the bank! Not one of her former fiancés would have stressed over a $3,000 liquor bill. That was the kind of money any one of them would have put out for her wedding shoes alone.

I was nervous knowing that even standing there, waiting for her in my tuxedo, Cynthia could still back out. I had heard that part of our pre-ceremony entertainment was a live performance by multi-platinum recording artist Kem, with a dance number by a ballerina. *I didn't see shit.* I was in a trance wondering if my elusive bride would meet me at the altar.

It felt like I stood there for hours, waiting for Cynthia to make her grand entrance. The room was moving in 3D slow motion. After about forty-five minutes, I saw her step out on a second-floor landing, but she quickly disappeared. I didn't see her or the camera crews for at least another hour. My heart was pounding a million beats a minute. Had she run off? I envisioned her jetting out the back door, climbing into a limo and telling the driver, *"Get me the fuck out of here!"* My mind was playing major tricks on me and the vodka only magnified my paranoia.

Out of nowhere, something from a higher place settled my thoughts and a peace came over my whole body. Cynthia's smile and reassuring words started to flash in my head like closed captioning on a screen. I could hear her voice whisper, *"I love you, Peter."* It reinvigorated me. I was reminded of how she put everything in her life aside to be with me in Georgia. Before the soothing thoughts could leave my head, Cynthia entered the room in a huge, steel-colored, silk gown. It was beautiful and flowing. I prayed she wouldn't fall in that big-ass dress and expensive Christian Louboutin shoes.

Other than the woman in that silver dress, nothing else mattered at that moment. Getting married under the Fernbank's prehistoric dinosaurs was symbolic for me because I knew we could last as long as them if we fought to stay together. With all we had endured to make that day happen, there would be nothing we couldn't conquer *together*.

Not one of her friends understood why she had left Manhattan for a ghetto-Jamaican who lived in country bumpkin Atlanta. She didn't live for them. *She lived for herself,* and she was consistently bold enough to do what her heart told her. Cynthia was a star who had met her king and everybody realized it on our wedding day.

I cried, with a part of me aching, because only God knew that I had not intentionally placed her in harm's way. I lost control of our finances and things had not turned out the way I imagined. I just wanted to marry the woman that I loved. I couldn't pay for her dream wedding, but she still loved me enough to show up. It was a moment in time I will never forget. She had so many options, but she rode with me. It is for that reason I will go hard for Cynthia Bailey until the day I die!

CHAPTER VI

Blackout Period
Our Financial Loss

Peter's At Capacity

OUR WEDDING TURNED out to be one of the most trying, yet happiest times of my life. I had finally married the woman who made my eyes cross from the first time I saw her. Unfortunately, my high hit the bricks when I saw the wedding episode of our show. I was mad as hell, watching Cynthia's mom and sister contemplate hiding our marriage license. It hit me hard. Not one of them had mentioned a word about it to me, *not even Cynthia.* When the shakedown aired, several months had already passed. Learning about the whole thing, along with the rest of the world, pissed me off even more.

Cynthia claimed she had no clue about what had gone on, because her mom and Malorie never brought it up. I wrestled with understanding how three women, who were so inseparable, had not ever discussed something so major. I was angry for a long time about it. It was embarrassing and painful for my parents to watch. Cynthia's mother and sister should have called a family meeting after the wedding and put their dirty laundry on the table. Hiding what they had done made it seem even more deceptive. They eventually apologized, but the situation still bothered me. I had no choice but to put it out of my mind, to make room for all the other shit that was falling apart around me.

The day I didn't have the strength to take out my keys and unlock the door, was the day I knew it was time to close Uptown. When I opened her, my vision was that she would be the hottest bar and dining scene in Atlanta. The interior was a custom build-out, with split stone on the wall, marbled fireplace and a $20,000 chandelier suspended in the main foyer. People would walk through the doors and feel like they had stepped into New York or Miami nightlife. Being seven months behind on my rent was proof enough that I couldn't go on. It was as if I had been holding onto a child that I could no longer afford to feed. I finally reached a point where I was prepared to give it to someone who had the means to nourish it.

My landlord was generous in a way that was unheard of in the business; I could always tell him the truth about what was going on with my finances. We agreed that I would stay on the lease until he found a replacement tenant. He allowed me to strip the space of most of my expensive upgrades. One of the biggest blessings was being able to keep my custom barstools and $7,500, Subzero wine coolers. It was his way of giving me an incentive to bow out graciously. We both had a feeling that a comeback was in my future, but neither of us knew when, where or how.

I tried to sell the chandelier on eBay, but it wasn't pulling in the type of bids I wanted. There were about a 100,000 others competing against it. I kept it stored in a corner of our garage for the longest time. I would look at it every day and ask, *"Why the hell won't you sell?"* The shit made me insanely depressed. Only one serious buyer came by to see it in person. He offered me only $3,000 for it. I told him to get the fuck out of dodge, and I closed my garage door in his face. I was broke, but I wasn't giving shit away like a crackhead looking for a fix. I would have eaten it before I sold it for chump change. That damn chandelier drove me crazy until the day Cynthia found a home for it – in the entrance of The Bailey Agency.

It's impossible for anyone to understand how tough it was for me to bounce back from the hit of our wedding *and losing Uptown.* In the beginning, Cynthia was a champ. She did a great job of stringing us along with the little bit of change she made for her first year on the show. I knew there would be financial advantages in doing another season, so I was always down to give the no-holds-barred version of our lives. Showing my ass every chance I got, put us in the lineup for Season 4, but it was a high price to pay at home.

Seeing myself angry and out of control was hard to stomach. Before our weekly show aired, we would always receive a preview disc a few days in advance. Sometimes my actions were so raw and humiliating, we wouldn't even want to watch the scenes again or answer the phone on the day the episode premiered. Cynthia would watch with her mouth wide opened and repeatedly ask, "Oh my God, Peter! Why did you do that? Why'd you say that?" She would cry every time.

What I saw as being true to my core, Cynthia perceived as unnecessary conflict and said it always forced her to put out fires that were started by my words. In my mind, that's what the shit was all about. Real drama. Real disputes. Real fallouts! My wife is just as strong as I am, but we don't show it in the same way. I wasn't as chill as some of the other husbands in the franchise, because I had a harder time shrugging things off. I have strong opinions and trying to hold them in eventually causes bigger problems. Even if I had managed to put the brakes on my attitude, the crews are skilled at picking up on little things; the cameras never lie, they expose.

I would constantly tell Cynthia that she had to toughen up. If we stopped believing in each other or hoping that things could get better, we would never get to the other side. Her bougie-ass friends (the types with hedge fund manager husbands), badgered her incessantly about joining

RHOA. They were determined to beat it in her head that she was above the show. They never missed an opportunity to let her know it wasn't too late to get out. Many stopped talking to her and completely disassociated themselves. Shit was upside down and everything in our lives needed fixing in some way or another.

Our intimacy was at the top of that repair list. I was stone cold in love with Cynthia and didn't want to be with anyone else. At night, her long legs would always find mine and she would lock them around me. I saw it as an indication that she still found comfort in me, but it was the only sign of her love for many months.

It was still up to me to find a way to turn our situation around. My pride wouldn't allow me to take handouts from anybody. Cynthia would stare through me every day with her beautiful, deep, brown eyes. The words never left her mouth but her sad eyes would ask, *"Peter, what are you going to do today to bail us out?"* I would answer her back with my eyes, *"Don't worry, baby. I'm going to get us out of this mess."* I knew I had to hit my Rolodex of movers and shakers to get my wheels in motion.

Vivian Scott Chew has been one of my closest friends for many years, and was even the best (wo)man in our wedding. Her husband, Ray Chew, is the musical conductor for *American Idol*. When we met, she was an executive for Sony Music. She's always been one of those sistas who's had my back from jump street. During the hard times after Cynthia and I got married, Vivian would always give me a heads up on opportunities in the industry or anything she thought could be a springboard for my comeback. She was a friend I could talk to about anything, *anytime.*

Leonard Burnett and Brett Wright (the co-owners of *UPTOWN Magazine*) had been my friends for over two decades. They were the pilot and co-pilot that helped me hold things down during those seriously shaky months. When I needed cash to make ends meet, I could pick up the phone and call either to spot me a few thousand. Leonard also allowed me to sell ad space for the magazine. He paid me a handsome commission for every sale, and gave me a $1,500 monthly retainer to serve as a consultant.

Another loyal supporter that kept me from going off the cliff was Heather Kenney. I could confide in her about any detail in my life and not hear back about it – which is rare in Atlanta. I met her when I was building Uptown, and I got a kick out of the fact that she was a lawyer who didn't practice law. She was educated, smart as hell and supported everything I did. When Uptown started slipping, she borrowed $20,000 from her dad and gave it to me to put back in the business.

Heather was a woman of means who came from a great family. Her father was a successful physician with several practices. She always knew if she needed anything, she could call home and get it. Real talk, she needed nothing from nobody. Out the gate, she and I were ride-or-die friends. People would always get it twisted, assuming we were more, but it was never anything else. It wasn't sexual or even a love interest, she was just a die-hard soldier who believed in my mission.

If I had five Heathers in my life, I'd be an unstoppable monster. She understood numbers well and how they interplayed in every aspect of running a business. She knew the more deals you stuck your damn nose in, the more bills you accumulated. So, between the two of us, we were always trying to scrape up change to make something pop off. Even when we would go out for happy hour, we went with the mindset of making a dollar out of fifteen cents. She would have twenty bucks, I would probably have even less, yet somehow the shit would always work out to be enough. Sometimes, people would recognize me and send rounds of drinks over to our table. Those were the sweet nights, because we would always leave with the money we walked in with.

The public perception was that I was Peter Thomas from *The Real Housewives of Atlanta*, so I had to be paid. Nothing was further from the truth, but I let people hold onto that image of me. It was a hell of a lot better than having my veins pumped with negative energy. I used their outlook as fuel to keep my motor running and get me and Cynthia back on top.

Cynthia's At Capacity

The night of our wedding, a friend secured a luxurious hotel suite for us, but we had just enough energy to make it home and drag ourselves into bed. Our wedding had been absolutely beautiful, but rather than being a day of fun memories, it ended up being another hurdle for us to jump. The whole planning phase was such a crazy roller coaster ride; I stayed in bed for two days sleeping away the physical and emotional drain. I slept all the time, even several weeks after our ceremony. I only left the house to do what I had to do. If it had not been for Noelle, I probably would have stayed in bed for months. I didn't want to be awake to face all the stuff that came along with pulling off our wedding. Sleeping became my escape.

When I awoke from my sleeping spell and didn't have the distraction of coordinating outfits, wigs, makeup and shooting schedules, anger began to set in. My inspiration for getting through the season had been making it to our wedding day and seeing the white production vans disappear from outside our house. The absence of all the chaos gave light to a mountain of debt and family drama. Malorie and my mother only added to our mounting stresses with their whole marriage certificate debacle. They never shared they had been filmed on our wedding day, having that conversation about hiding our certificate.

Just days before the RHOA episode showing the details aired, Peter and I watched it unfold in the privacy of our home. I was speechless and he was furious. He refused to hear that I had no part in the matter. It upset me that

Peter and his family were hurt by my mother and Mal's gullibility. I was also sad for my mother and sister. They were good-natured and caring people who would never have done anything to hurt Peter or me. They got caught up in the moment and were unfortunately captured in a very vulnerable and unflattering perspective. The scene showed what they did, but it wasn't an accurate depiction of who they were as human beings.

Our money situation was a whole different stressor. Realizing the condition of our finances was petrifying! After relocating to Atlanta, most of my time had been devoted to working on the show. Living in Georgia decreased my flexibility to go on casting calls. I no longer had the luxury of hopping on a plane and going to New York as I did before. Uptown was no more, and we were struggling to stay above water. Some days, it was a nearly impossible feat just to keep the basics covered.

No one had a clue of how bad things were, and those who knew took a lot of comfort in our misery. The responsibility of paying a $3,500 mortgage and other household obligations made it a difficult road. My only security was knowing our car was paid off and we would at least have reliable transportation. My faith told me if we could maintain a roof over our heads, everything else would work out.

Some people are the kind of broke where they lose their house and move in with someone else. We were the kind that wasn't homeless and on the streets, but God knows we struggled to keep our home. Things were tighter than I had ever experienced as an adult. We could buy groceries, just not what we were accustomed to stocking in our pantry. Noelle's Froot Loops were replaced with Hoop Loops. She hated them! I didn't want to rip the Tiffany spoon from her mouth and make her feel the consequences of our poor choices, but I did what was necessary to keep us going. I tried to soften the blow by creating fun ways to budget and improvise.

We played a game of "Let's Not Go to the Grocery Store Until the Refrigerator Is Empty." The object of the game would be to eat everything from the freezer and refrigerator before going shopping again. It was my way of stretching our money, with as little impact as possible to Noelle. Even at the grocery store, I would go out of my way to make it fun for her. I'd say, "Okay, let's see how much we can buy with $60." I took a creative approach to all things regarding Noelle and our finances. Instead of going to Barnes & Noble and buying ten books – we would sit in the store, read two and buy one. That is, until the day Noelle let me off the hook, telling me I didn't have to take her to the bookstore because she knew I couldn't afford it. It didn't feel good to realize that she had figured everything out on her own.

I had no idea how to explain what had happened to her seemingly normal life. One of the first times Noelle saw me cry came from watching me on the show. It was excruciating for her because she had always seen me as a pillar of strength. I hated her seeing me upset, so I made her stop watching. There was also some negativity in scenes involving my mom and sister; Noelle's restriction eliminated the issue of her having to deal with those things. It would have just confused her more.

I am a simple girl, who didn't come from much, but I learned to think on my feet. I moved from the Alabama country life to New York City, had a child and worked around the world while raising her. I made something out of nothing, but I had entered a stifling space – where I couldn't recreate. I was angry at Peter, angry at myself and frustrated with all the stupid decisions we'd made with our money. I had always been able to take on a lot, but when you're down and out, it's hard to see the brighter side of things. It was the first time in my life I remember whining or feeling sorry for myself. I was starting over.

That time was the ultimate test of my marriage. I had so many doubts about Peter. In many ways, I blamed him for everything. He was the one who had convinced me to move to Atlanta, be on the show and take risks I was never comfortable with. He was the kind of man who could wake up with a dollar in his pocket and walk around all day like he was Barack

Obama. It was the very reason I loved and disliked him. I didn't know how to be that way. When I was broke, I felt like it, acted like it, looked like it and probably smelled like it!

Our relationship was on serious life support. In my mind, I had bought what I thought was a expensive Picasso, only to find it was a fake with a thousand other copies selling for $10 at the flea market. We barely talked, and when we did it would end in an argument. I didn't want to hear shit about the *"glass being half full…keeping hope alive…"* and all the other stuff he was preaching! I was miserable and wanted him to be miserable too.

I held him responsible for ripping my world apart, and I was determined to drive him away. I figured he would leave if I hurt him in every way I knew how. He had given up the least, so if one of us had to leave, it would be him. He finally packed his things and left, *for a week*. I thought he would be happier without me, but he wasn't. He called and said he wanted to come home. I missed him too, so much so that it pissed me off even more! How the hell do you miss a man that you ran off? I had tried my best to make him feel my pain, but it never worked. Peter loved me through it all and refused to go down that road. Had he gone, I would have probably hated him for that too. He was damned if he did and damned if he didn't.

We endured some brutal times, but I found out that Peter Thomas is a man, by every measure. I don't think any other man in my life had ever been more passionate about being with me. In our worst moments, Peter still wanted to hold my hand, cuddle with me and make love to me. I was so closed off that I didn't see how sex could make things better. If the conversation didn't end in how we could catch up on a bill, then I didn't want to have it! The Cynthia Bailey sex factory was closed. I just shut everything down so we would both be good and miserable. Don't get it twisted now, I married a man who puts in down in the bedroom, I was just too unhappy to take myself there. I was horrible! I don't know how Peter managed to get through it all.

I had felt so alone and disheartened that I didn't care about anything. I shut out my friends and didn't want to hear anybody's shitty advice. The only person I gave myself to was Noelle, but looking back, I shut down on her too. I couldn't even be depressed like I wanted! My responsibilities as a mom still required me to carpool and help with homework, which made me angrier. I was like, *"Damn, can't a bitch just have a nervous breakdown?"* God would not allow it, and made Noelle my motivation for getting back.

Peter's Oxygen Mask

Even though I knew the music industry well and had a lot of contacts, for months I was going nowhere fast. Over the years the music business had turned, and most artists would never even see a tenth of the sales that an album like "Thriller" had achieved. I put feelers out to The Jamaican Tourist Board, Russell Simmons and anyone else who would listen to my ideas. I had a vision to create an international music conference that would bring reggae back to music's forefront. Unfortunately, there was no real organized publishing in Jamaica and piracy was at an all-time high. One door after another was getting slammed in my face.

I prayed to God every day to turn our lives round. I was fifty years old, broke *and broken.* On a trip out to Jamaica, I got real sick and called for a doctor to come to my room. I couldn't shake the feeling that I was going to die there alone. As sick as I was, I got up, caught a plane and took my ass home. I hated the feeling of returning from a business meeting and walking back through that door empty handed. I felt like less of a man, and that I was letting Cynthia down.

I rose every morning before daylight and hit the road looking under every boulder I could lift. Things had gotten so bad, I had to ask Cynthia for gas money to go out and look for opportunities. I was still the father of five, and my responsibilities didn't disappear just because I didn't have the money. I couldn't ask my wife to take care of my children or make my child support payments. The worst feeling was not being able to provide if my kids needed something. I wanted to burst, but I knew it wouldn't help anything.

The Christmas following our wedding, I went to California to visit my middle daughter, Blaze. We went to The Grove shopping mall, and I had about $300 in my pocket to last the whole trip. The father in me couldn't help but ask if she needed anything. I prayed it wouldn't be too outrageous.

When I asked, she just stared into my face like an old soul and said, "No, Daddy, I don't need anything. I'm just glad you're here. If you want, you can buy me a book." It was the one thing I knew I could afford. I almost sprained my damn ankle running to the nearest bookstore. My two girls were very mature and understood my situation. It gave me a deeper sense of faith just hearing them say, "Everything will get better, Daddy."

The sky opened up the day Kandi Burruss passed along info to Cynthia about a guy named Al, who was looking for someone to take over a defunct space he owned. The occupying tenants were running a Mexican restaurant and had not paid rent in years. Al wanted a new renter to come in and flip the spot into a thriving restaurant and bar. When Cynthia told me about the opportunity, I didn't like the idea. I wasn't interested in doing a bar concept. I later learned that Al was a New Yorker and an entrepreneur who owned several businesses. I figured I at least owed him the courtesy of a meeting.

When I went to see the place, it had eight bottles of liquor behind the bar and six customers in the whole damn restaurant. The interior of the space was laid out in a way that didn't allow it to breathe. It was like a jail, with all views to the outside obstructed. I immediately saw how it could be better. One of my God-given talents is taking ugly ducklings and turning them into functional, beautiful swans. I could walk into any space with four walls and know its exact potential. That shithole was no different.

I talked to Cynthia about the possibility of me stepping in as the new owner. She thought it was a good idea but made it clear she had no money to fund the project. I understood her hesitation and convinced a close friend to put up $45,000. I told him his investment would go toward a modest face-lift. I was afraid to let him know the build-out would cost three times the amount of the money he fronted. I needed to keep his interest piqued and anxiety down. Al was hella down and supported me in getting things off the ground by adding his own $40,000 to the pot.

I wanted to do a tapas menu and focus more on alcohol than food. Pulling it off wouldn't be easy, but if anyone had the will do it, I did. I scraped, borrowed, and hard-money loaned my way to raising another $200,000. Cynthia came up with a name, and ten months from the date of my first visit, we opened bar ONE. It was a feeling that words couldn't do justice.

After our first season of *The Real Housewives* wrapped, I had spent so many days feeling like the most worthless and hated man on television. I was unspeakably deflated and had willed myself to admitting that I needed to gracefully let go of Cynthia. People had labeled me a failure that misspent his wife's money and lost his business. Starting a new undertaking made me feel alive again! It was the first time since saying our marital vows that I felt Cynthia wanted to stay with me to repair our finances *and our marriage.*

Hitting rock bottom made the air smell even fresher on the way back up. Only a few people knew all the details on how low we had sunk, but from watching the show, anyone could see we had run out of money. As a result, people saw me and Cynthia as prototypes of how to go about getting your life back after a meltdown. We knew what mistakes not to repeat. If we could make peanut butter out of the peanuts she had earned from her first season, we could do wonders with the second season money.

When that first *real* check came for her sophomore season, we didn't use it to ball out. We invested in shit that could yield returns. We weren't brand new, we were grownups! We put a budget in place to make the money last until the next check, which we knew would arrive nine months later. We didn't squander one dime or leave any details to chance or luck. It was a relief realizing if nothing else, we had enough to pay our household bills. We already lived in a comfortable, beautiful home and it got even cozier knowing we could keep the lights on.

The day bar ONE opened in October 2011, the public was breaking down the doors to get in. Though we opened mid-month, our profits were good and got better as time progressed. By that December, we had enough excess to pay off all our debt (including the money we borrowed from Cynthia's mother for our wedding), and The Bailey Agency was born. Cynthia didn't contribute money to bar ONE, but she told me there would always be a stash put aside if I needed it. With all we had survived, she hated seeing me ask people for money. She still had my back, because she knew I would break mine to support anything she ever aspired to do.

My sense of gratitude toward people grew in a way that I had never experienced. I took pride in working in my business each night, going to every table and greeting the guests. I'd hold a conversation or take pictures with anyone who was interested. I went out of my way to let customers know how much I appreciated them being there. They loved the service, and in return would come back and always bring new friends. My best moments were when customers would tell me how Cynthia and I inspired them. Even men who watched the show could relate to our pain and suffering. It was an energy that propelled me to another level, because I had never seen myself as a role model for anyone.

People, who get a chance to know me, love me. But love me or hate me, my mission has always been to use our celebrity to secure a solid future for us. If millions of people know our names, Cynthia and I should have a business plan that earns $10 from each one. We refuse to let our story end like a lot of people who walked away from the franchise without shit to show for their breech of privacy.

Cynthia and I have really been blessed. I am a pretty normal dude whose wife just happens to be the hottest chick on the planet. Our blackout period made me more normal *and humble*. Even in our darkest moment, I always believed that Cynthia and I could turn our lives around, because of who we were and still are! To this day, I continue to relish in that feeling of being revitalized. If you get close enough, you might even be able to smell the comeback on my breath. How sweet it is!

Cynthia's Oxygen Mask

Why the hell couldn't I fall apart for just once in my life? I had never been a quitter or a pessimist. For most of my life, I'd held together a *picture-perfect* silhouette for the world. I was always the girl who could never be a disaster – Little Miss Perfect. In my desert, I still had to care for my child, clean my house and appear to be happy *when I wasn't*.

Peter taught me that not having money doesn't mean you aren't rich. Not being able to provide for us devastated him, but he was a man who refused to be measured by what was in his pocket. He forced people to judge him by his abilities. His outlook on Uptown was a perfect example of how he viewed things. He never saw Uptown as a failure; it was simply a business venture that didn't succeed, so he moved on to the next thing. After watching him lose his business on television, nobody gave him love. For months, nothing he touched would take off. Every day brought a new and bigger obstacle, but he always stayed up.

His feet never touched the bottom! While I hibernated, he came out fighting like Muhammad Ali. Being around me was a constant downer, so he'd stay gone for the better part of the day. I was like a negative hater who tested his faith every chance I got. I wanted the comfort of at least knowing our mortgage would be paid. I would nag him relentlessly about our prospect of returning to the show, "What if we're not asked back? What if the check doesn't come in time to save our house?" He always reassured me that we would be invited back, and if not, something better would come along.

I didn't want to talk to Malorie or my mother, because I'd already gotten them involved beyond what was appropriate. Telling them too much was the very reason they started feeling *some type of way* about Peter. I only wanted to talk with the other women on the show about what I was going through. They could empathize with my agony. NeNe was an ally and confidante. More than anyone, she understood the challenges I was facing. She knew the stresses of losing all sense of privacy and exposing your relationship to the universe. She shared that Peter and I were very much like she and Gregg, as they had winged it their first season too.

She always made me feel like quitting or not getting through it wasn't an option. She told me that Peter and I had gone too far to just turn it off. She was right! You can't become un-famous! You can leave the show, but people will still know you. Had I quit, I would have regretted not returning for the rest of my life. I shared a lot with NeNe, but I never fully opened up about how bad our situation had become. I was still getting to know her and was terrified she might turn on me and broadcast our hardships world.

Why did I have to be the strong one? I felt like everything was resting on me. Returning to *The Real Housewives* was ultimately my choice, because Peter couldn't be on the show without me. Our future hinged on whatever decision I made. One day, I awoke numb to all the peering eyes and judgments against Peter and me. I decided I was going to cross the finish line, regardless of what people thought. I stopped caring about everyone else's opinions and took only our wants and needs into account. Peter was already on the page and jumped right in. I was the late bloomer, *again*. I had been so beaten down I wouldn't allow him to talk to me about winning, because we seemed to be losing in every aspect of our lives.

Soon after, I got the Bravo email inviting me back for a second season. There is always the possibility of the least-desirable or least-favored housewives being replaced with new, more interesting ones. I was actually happy to receive the invitation, but sad to take that train again with all its unpredictable stops. I still doubted if I was even emotionally strong enough to return. Peter played a big role in getting my mind in the right place, and before I knew it my lawyer was negotiating my new contract. It's a process that can take a day, a week or even months. Our situation was so tight; I couldn't afford to negotiate for more than a couple of days.

To date, our wedding show has been the highest-rated RHOA finale. It gave me leverage to ask for the compensation I felt I deserved. I had paid a big price my first season, yet had earned very little money that year, and most of my earnings were spent before they even hit my bank account. During our hiatus, we struggled to stay above water but couldn't get afloat. I did some hosting appearances and a Macy's commercial, but we never managed to do better than barely survive. The second time around, we knew we needed a solid strategy to get the number we wanted.

After all we had sacrificed, if I couldn't get a fair deal, I was willing to walk away. I saw myself as a unique addition to the cast, particularly with my secret weapon, *Peter Thomas*. Who in the world can serve up a hot plate of Peter, but Peter? Needless to say, we stuck to our number and got it! After finalizing and signing off on my new contract, a big chunk of the money hit my account the very next day. We had not paid our mortgage in several months, and were just nine days away from having our home auctioned off on the courthouse steps. We were so far behind, we had to take a cashier's check directly to the mortgage company's attorney to stop the foreclosure proceedings.

We didn't want to lay out all our cards and risk being kicked off the show, but had absolutely teetered on the very edge of disaster. It was one thing to lose a business on television, but another to lose your home and have your belongings put out on the street. Had one thing gone wrong or my check come one week later, our story would have probably had a much different ending.

Getting the advance for our second season put us in a more peaceful place. We caught up every bill that was behind, and Noelle finally got to put a box of real Froot Loops in the grocery basket. People say money doesn't make you happy, but being broke shole don't either.

After the smoke cleared from our financial combustion, Peter and I finally sat down and had a heart-to-heart talk. Months before, I wasn't in the mood to talk about anything that didn't have zeros behind it! I was more focused on our recovery than anything else. Quite honestly, I didn't really miss the physical aspect of our relationship as much as I missed communicating with him. It was good to be able to have a conversation with my husband, less the river of anger. We weren't back at *booed up* status, but we were talking to each other in complete sentences again.

We both were in monster business mode and used a portion of the money to start new projects. When we lost our money, we lost our power. My priority was to create several outlets that would make us money, because money represented power *and freedom.* I started my agency and Peter opened a smaller lounge, bar ONE. I didn't invest in it, but I held back money in case he ever needed emergency funds.

Being in a phase where we barely had money to buy food and pay utilities was beyond frightening for me. Not coming from money, I had always been very careful with spending and managing it. I ran from being poor by living on a budget for most of my life, no matter how much money I made. I had to force myself to splurge on big-ticket items. Peter didn't have that gene. It was hard for him to gauge when his tank was nearing E. He had the attitude that money would always come his way, no matter what.

It was hard to change a fifty-year-old's thought pattern, but I was willing to die trying. He now understands that he works best with a budget because it helps him be accountable. By the time he comes to me for his reserve, I know he's exhausted every option, outside of robbing a convenient store. We're both comfortable with my role as the house banker.

Peter knows if I'm taking care of the money, we'll always have some put back. He's made it very clear to me that if he had millions, I would still be the house treasurer. It's a formula that works for us.

Dark times make the good times great! I never believed anything that emotionally and financially devastating could happen to me. I didn't realize it, but I had taken many aspects of my life and fortune for granted. The rise and fall, and rise again, made me appreciate being able to fill up my tank without having to watch the gage. I remember the days of halting the pump at $10. I didn't know that feeling before marrying Peter. In fact, I truly had forgotten how much things cost. The school of hard knocks taught me the price of an avocado and a gallon of gas.

The human spirit can accomplish wonders when it's backed into a corner. If we could win in business, it would also be a victory for our marriage. I had never run a company before opening my school, but I completely trusted Peter as a business man. Knowing my vulnerabilities, he did a great job of guiding me in launching my first venture. Staying in unison eventually got us back in the bedroom. My attraction to Peter had always been that he was a smart and a dangerous risk-taker. With him, you either hit the jackpot or lose it all to the house!

Relief arrived the day I gave it all up to God and trusted that I was exactly where He wanted me to be. It took me a long time to surrender to the notion, but as I was able to let go, the battle got easier every day. My attitude about money has been forever altered. In our storm, my one extravagance was getting a manicure, but I would always get the basic service. To this day, I appreciate the luxury of being able to go in and have my nails done professionally, instead of doing them myself. I still get the regular and sometimes forget I can afford to pay that extra $15 for a deluxe.

I love Peter for seeing me through my time of gloom. He kept nurturing and caring for me with the force of a tornado. There were moments when I couldn't stand the sight of him. I had to argue, cry, shout and pray to get back to my place as his loving wife. It took a while, but I managed to completely forgive him and share in the responsibility of our failures.

Peter never held a gun to my head or forced my hand to do anything. Everything I did, I had done willingly.

Those dark days resulted in the highly favored existence we now share. Peter loved me at my best and worst. Anybody else would've left *and stayed gone*. I still don't know how he did it, but I learned that Peter really and truly cannot be broken. I had his heart, and if anyone can break you, it's the one you give your heart to. He taught me I'm a lot tougher than I thought I was. If I die tomorrow, the one thing I will know for sure is that Peter Thomas loved me.

I am humbled.

I am grateful.

I am thankful.

I am truly blessed!

CHAPTER VII

Overbooked
Our Exes & Careers

Cynthia's Double-Booked

HAVING WORKED AS a model for most of my life, with each year getting better, I thought it was something I could do forever. I never contemplated life after modeling, until I became pregnant with Noelle. After learning of her impending arrival, everyone seemed to have more questions about my and Leon's future together than we'd ever had ourselves. I was pressed about whether I'd become a stay-at-home mom, maintain residency in New York or move to California where Leon worked most of the time. Setting a wedding date would have made our parents extremely happy, but it had no bearing on our happiness.

Leon and I thoroughly discussed becoming parents, and agreed we were responsible enough to raise a child outside of marriage. We weren't just lovers – we were best friends who loved each other. I'm a straight fool anytime I'm in love. It puts me in a state where not much else matters. I could be living in a castle with a tower or a shack with an outhouse – as long as it's real and with the right man, I'm good. Leon was a great dad and partner, but I never saw marriage as something that needed to occur just because we had a child. I remember taking the pregnancy test and asking myself if I could feed another mouth, even without Leon in the picture. The answer was yes.

It's a blessing to find someone you sincerely care about and enjoy spending your days with. You become bold enough to erase boundaries and allow your heart to have what it wants. From the first time I met Leon, I knew he was supposed to be in my life forever. Something spoke to me and said he would be the man to father my child. Everything about him felt so right; it didn't even make sense. I loved his parents, his family and anything connected to him. From the time my e.p.t. revealed a positive result, I moved in with him. It felt incredible to take the journey of parenthood together.

Before my pregnancy, my life had been dominated by my work and travel schedule. Once I became a mom, I wanted to be on the road less and in New York as often as possible. I treasured one-on-one quality time with Noelle, but I struggled to balance being home and working to maintain the lifestyle we were accustomed to living. The daily dilemma of deciding whether to continue working, get married or relocate out west started to take its toll on me. I had no formula to determine how much change in my life was necessary, just because I'd had a child.

Leon became more consistent with the addition of a child to our equation, but motherhood changed me drastically. The fine, sexy, spontaneous Cynthia evaporated. Low-cut dresses went to the back of the closet and comfortable mom's jeans became the order of the day. I was less of a fun girlfriend and more of a mom. I didn't know how to be a lover and a mother at the same time. It was hard to turn off my mommy switch and get back to how Leon and I had been before our baby.

Even if we were on a romantic private island, I never allowed myself to be more than a stone's throw from my cell phone. Leon would always tell me that he had a baby, but lost his girl. It was the shameful truth! The girl who would've jumped off a cliff with him and asked questions later, was gone. My life's mission became being the best mom I could be, and Noelle was my single focus.

By the time she was a year old, Leon and I had purchased a home together in Montclair, New Jersey. We were forced to take inventory of our relationship around the three-year mark. We pursued the answer to the nagging question of whether marriage would have organically occurred between us if there had been no Noelle. As partners, we knew we could not have been more compatible – both artists, Pisces and free spirits. We were attracted to the parts of ourselves that we saw in the other, but those same things ultimately contributed to our downfall.

Our similarities made it easy to maintain harmony in our relationship, but over time, they became stagnating blockages. When two artists get together, there's such a lack of contrast, they eventually start to drown in a sea of likeness. On the contrary, with an artist and an entrepreneur (like me and Peter), the multitude of differences force both to grow in new ways. The business mind pushes the artistic spirit beyond its comfort zone and vice versa. Visionaries often see creative people bigger than they're able to see themselves. Left to our own devices, people like Leon and me would easily get stuck in a cycle of only doing what we liked or what felt good.

My destiny was to take the passage of parenthood with Leon. The belief that our paths were supposed to intersect made it easier to walk away when I knew it was over. Leon was the man who brought out the *jet off to Europe for a month and live off the land* side of me. We did every single possible thing a couple in love could have done. Leon needed attention and special moments with me. I hated that I could no longer give him what he had signed up for.

He was not a guy who could find contentment in sitting around the house twiddling his thumbs. He was a good man who always followed what was right; a flower child who loved life and venturing out into the world. He will never die of anything stress-related. He is a happy, peaceful man who lives a happy, peaceful life. He viewed marriage as an honorable next step, but it wasn't the right move or right time for me.

I thought that leaving him was the mature way of acknowledging that we were done. Looking back, it was very selfish, and I wished I'd used a more compassionate approach. My decision to breakup with him was agonizing, but I felt letting go would be doing him a favor. It turned out to be the best thing not only for me and Leon, but also for our child. Simply put, Noelle became the love of my life. He lost me to her, but sharing our precious daughter made me feel that I had not lost him.

I'm a low-maintenance woman with complicated angles. I could never see myself in a relationship that didn't work for both partners. I'd always tried to pick companions who held the same belief. My mode of operation was to walk in the front door of a relationship looking for the back door. I needed to know there would always be a way out of whatever I got into. My biggest fear is being blissfully stuck *in anything* – a hairstyle, job and most definitely a relationship. Most people stay long after it's over because they find comfort in familiarity, good sex, financial security or fame. I only want to be where my soul tells me to take root. If a relationship does not add to my personal happiness, I no longer find it appealing.

Truthfully, some part of my separation with Leon may have had to do with me being a loner at heart. I had traveled the world as a solo act, walked the streets of Paris by myself and actually enjoyed dinner and a movie without a plus one. Not being in a relationship wasn't the kiss of death my single girlfriends made it out to be. Going through life without getting married or having a kid wasn't the worst thing that could have happened to a woman. I kept the attitude that it would be a blessing if it materialized, but if it didn't…*oh well!* I admit, though, every now and again the thought of waking up old and alone scared the crap out of me.

Peter's Double-Booked

When the bottom dropped out of my and Cynthia's banking accounts, it wasn't my first trip to the trenches. After I had separated from the mother of my youngest child, Bryce Hernandez, I left Miami for the first time in eighteen years. Construction projects up and down South Beach had slowed business to a near halt. I lost all my money trying to wait out the storm, literally. After Hurricane Katrina struck in 2005, my beachside bar was losing money like a piggy bank with a hole in his belly. My landlord initiated a lease for a tenant who agreed to take over my space, as well as the one above it. In return, he gave me $100,000 to hand over my keys and evacuate. *Sound familiar?*

I collected the money in two parts and used the first $50,000 to secure a lease on a hair salon for Bryce's mom. She was a gorgeous woman and talented stylist with an incredible personality. Her clientele loved her enough to follow her wherever she went. I knew she was miserable working at the shop where she rented space, so I used the opportunity to capitalize on her beauty and make her the face of a new salon.

We were cash poor, so it took me eight months to renovate a building that should have only taken three. I did all the teeth-grinding, grunge work and oversaw the shoestring budget for the project. My ex gave me hardly any appreciation for my sweat and sacrifice. I put my money and effort into creating something that would satisfy her needs, and she wouldn't even dedicate time to scouting out a location.

In relationships, I prefer doing things as a team. Working together allows both partners to feel a sense of achievement when success comes. I never liked lopsided equations, where one person did all the work, and the other took all the credit. In my eyes, couples who set goals, worked as a unit and appreciated each other's talents, exemplified something solid. I was on my back by the time I discovered a lot of people aren't wired that way. Ten years later, I'm still on the hook as a cosigner for my ex, but her position remains that I did nothing for her. Her lack of gratitude stabbed me in the heart and put me in an emotional dungeon.

In the beginning, I was crazy about her. In the end, it was a *Nightmare on Elm Street* situation. When we met, everything on the business front was hot for me. After Katrina struck, I wasn't bouncing like she was accustomed. Seeing her interest fade, made her seem fake and materialistic. While the contempt in our relationship intensified, we were building a business, a million-dollar home and expecting a baby. It had been twenty years since the birth of my first child, and I was excited when I found out she was carrying a boy. I never missed one doctor's appointment.

As tensions got tighter, we drifted further apart in our home life. My coping mechanism was to hold it all in. I had a tendency to internalize things, because I believed a man should never share certain details with a woman. It was a lethal mistake that would lead her to think she had him figured out and eventually make her feel entitled to start speaking on his behalf. I wasn't cool with anybody talking for me, not even my woman. So I caught the brick, sucked it up and kept it all to myself.

By the time Bryce was a year old, we had moved into our new home and her salon was about 90 percent done. So much irreversible shit had happened in the relationship, I had to go. She was going in a different direction and it wasn't with me. When we officially made the split, she was already seeing someone else. *Our breakup was nuts.* I ran out of South Beach before I did something I knew I would regret for the rest of my life.

Toronto was my first option. I'd made a name for myself there, and I knew it would be easy to set up meetings with key people. Years before, I'd held my "How Can I Be Down" music conference in Miami, and a quarter of the registrants were from Toronto. The conference featured A&R, publishing information and a panel of industry experts for people interested in the business. A friend who lived in Toronto encouraged me to come up and get my mojo back. It was a good look for me; especially since I wanted to get as far away as possible from my ex. I didn't want to be in the same city, state *or country* with her.

While I was in Canada, she had her new guy move into the house we built together. I'd had plenty of experience in recognizing when a woman was done and didn't want to be with a man anymore. Her actions motivated me to stay away for the next six months and work like hell. On the first day of the Toronto "How Can I Be Down" convention, the blizzard of 2006 hit. It stretched all the way down to New York City. It was a miracle that the conference was able to clear $60,000. It was just enough to get me back to the States and create a new lane.

I still couldn't see myself sharing the same zip code with my ex, so I went to Los Angeles and spent time with my daughter Blaze and her mom. As much as I liked being around them, I couldn't get comfortable in their world. Blaze's mom gave me the impression that she wanted us to have another shot. I loved her deeply and didn't want to hurt her, but I needed a clean slate. I didn't belong in California. In March of 2007, I made my way to Atlanta.

Cynthia's City Pair

Even though I wasn't big on celebrating birthdays, I felt there was something monumental about turning forty. It was one of those seasons in my life that I knew I was on the verge of major change. Meeting Peter was the first time since Leon that I thought, *"Okay, here comes another train I need to catch."* For years I had not been even remotely intrigued by a man, but my intuition told me Peter was different. My attraction and feelings toward him were undeniable, and I knew what it meant. The only problem was that he lived in Georgia, and I lived in New York.

My premonition of a life metamorphosis turned out to be a Dionne Warwick Psychic Friends Network prediction. That year I met Peter, moved to Atlanta and joined *The Real Housewives of Atlanta*. My bookers, agents and friends were baffled by my seemingly sudden decision to uproot my life. New York was home for Leon, Noelle and I. Relocating, would make it inconvenient for Leon to continue building a relationship with his daughter. It didn't make me feel good that I was taking his only child to another state. We had a mature conversation about my decision to move, and being the reasonable man he had always been, Leon gave me his blessing. As co-parents, I still appreciated and respected his input. His approval was important, but getting to Atlanta with Peter was just as vital.

Peter and Leon are very different men and could not be more of a night-and-day comparison. Leon and I had more of a spiritual connection, where we could finish each other's sentences. He could always sense when something was off with me. Our focus was always on staying inspired and feeling good. Peter is my husband and the love of my life, not necessarily my soul mate. Our focus is on building a future and living good.

Peter and I are not ideally compatible, but we are ideal partners. Our outlooks radically differ, so we work well together and complement each other. Regardless of whether Peter's concepts fail or succeed, he always knows how and when to put the next deal together. He has a shrewd brain that consistently figures out how to make money without working for someone else. I haven't met many business people who share his ability to finagle out of a sticky situation. His Houdini precision has educated me in ways I probably could not have accessed if we hadn't met.

My first lesson in his life class was witnessing him steer us though the unpredictable recession. It hit six months after I got to Atlanta, and it felt like somebody had pushed the pause button on my career. Retailers were making massive changes in their processes and cutting back. Exotic location shoots turned into fabricated studio sets. Lucrative catalog sessions slowed down, and five-day bookings were compressed into two. Most of the black girls were the first to go. Typically, when you look at a Macy's, Talbots or Nordstrom catalog, the majority of the models on the pages are not women of color. So when cuts were mandated, there were even less of us working. My phone stopped ringing, and I was worried about getting work of any kind, much less modeling.

The decline in my workload had Peter and I even more excited about the potential of Uptown. We'd hoped my free time could be used helping to grow and manage the business. We saw the worst-case scenario as us having a beautiful restaurant that we could run as equals. We had done our research and realized that not only did people go out and drink during recessions, they drank more. We actually thought we could get through the downturn unscathed. When Uptown washed away, the tide of the recession swept away a lot of other stuff with it.

I tried to shift gears and turn my attention toward something based in the Atlanta fashion industry. I considered becoming a buyer or working on the corporate creative side at an upscale retailer like Neiman's or Saks. I figured with my expertise, I could transition into the role of an art director or a figurehead who decided fashion trends. I just knew some savvy businessperson would give me a fair shot and see me as a win-win addition to their organization. The stark reality was the people in Atlanta who held those jobs had degrees in fashion, I didn't.

In New York, you could get a gig off the street, strictly on talent. I was consistently hired based on the strength of my resume, rather than a distinction printed on a degree. In Georgia, being Cynthia Bailey and having twenty-five years of experience as a model meant nothing. I couldn't muster the energy to resell myself to an industry that I'd worked in for most of my life. As you age, you're less open to change. Career changes happen a lot easier for a twenty-something year old than it does a forty-something year old. If a decision maker couldn't sit across from me and see the possibilities

I represented, their business was not a place I wanted to be. Needless to say, the pursuit of my corporate retail endeavors was short-lived.

Before I could calculate my next move, the RHOA casting came about and the rest is history as we now know it. Even then, the artist in me only wanted to do what gave me goose bumps. Peter, who always looked at everything as a business deal, saw it differently. He planted the seed of how the opportunity was a conceivable business model. Once the show aired, our fame was a quick and weird realization. Usually people become famous when they star in a blockbuster movie or write a hit song, but on a reality show you're famous for simply being on television. I had worked my whole life using my face, but *Housewives* made my mildly familiar face a household name.

Tons of opportunities came along with my newfound celebrity, some in the unlikeliest forms. On our second season reunion show, I wore a long wavy weave. The demand for the look was so popular that I was approached to start my own line of hair extensions.

Like any other accessory, I love using wigs and weaves to complete my look. In the beginning, Bravo found it problematic because no other housewife changed her look as frequently as I did. I think they wanted every housewife to have a signature look that was consistent and recognizable. They also wanted to ensure that our hair changes didn't create character confusion for the viewers; especially in my case, since going from short hair to a longer weave completely altered my appearance.

I understood their logic, but the monotony of sporting the same 'do didn't work for me. I had worked in an alternate universe where changing your hairstyle was as common as a McDonald's sitting on every street corner in America. Social media, editorial and fan responses to my styling choices quickly made believers out of the producers. Now, my hairstyles are like wardrobe changes and one of the elements most-loved about me. Andy Cohen, the host of our reunion shows, also became a fan of my ever-changing styles and began to look forward to what trend I would be rocking.

Of all the doors that opened as a result of the show, the biggest opportunity was the one I created for myself by opening The Bailey Agency. It stretched my aptitude and sensibilities as a businesswoman. As a model, my agents sought out my clients and managed every aspect of the deal for me. With my school, my fate rests completely in my own hands.

The best and most brilliant advice for diversifying my business came from my now-friend, Russell Simmons. He advised me to open a fashion school instead of a modeling agency. *His advice was priceless.* True model material (someone who has the potential to actually make money and have a career) is only about one in every fifty students. Atlanta is still a developing market and has very little local work. There are a lot of beautiful and unique faces floating about, but the consistent modeling work is based out of Miami, Los Angeles and New York. Launching The Bailey Agency as a school allowed more students to receive training and education, and the concept generated a lot more overall business.

Originally, I thought we'd be catering to teenagers. I wasn't focused on little kids, but children have grown to represent a big part of our business. Having a school versus an agency accomplishes my main goal of not turning anyone away who has a heart geared toward fashion. We have created many avenues and programs to motivate and inspire every individual that crosses our threshold.

Most people come with the hopes of becoming a high-fashion model, but because they may not meet a size or height requirement, they often end up entering a pageant or taking acting classes. As long as a person's endeavors mildly relate to fashion or entertainment, The Bailey Agency has the means to cultivate them. Launching a school would've probably been a natural transition for me at some point in my life, but being on the show motivated me to do it quicker.

Our brand and impact continue to grow with the success of the Miss Renaissance Pageant, The Cynthia Bailey Model Search and the upcoming release of my Cynthia Bailey doll. I am living my life's dreams while nurturing the aspirations of so many others. In a couple of years I'll pinch myself, but right now, I'm just not ready to wake up.

Peter's City Pair

My parents were two people in the world who had my back no matter how many times life threw a dagger my way. My move to Georgia could not have been timed more perfectly. My dad underwent triple bypass surgery, and my brother thought it was a good idea that I come to Atlanta and help care for him. Even as he suffered through his own healing, my dad cared enough to soothe the emotional wounds left open from my recent breakup. Being around and talking to him was like free therapy. He empathized over how much I missed my young son. I already had four kids who didn't live with me, and I didn't want Bryce to be another. If I'd had any idea that his mom and I weren't built to last, I would never have had a child with her.

I had very little time to lick my wounds in Atlanta. My first priority was to find a new spot to do my thing. My brother Earl kept telling me that Atlanta needed something fresh and gave me the idea for Uptown. I only had $60,000 (from my venture in Toronto) and every dime needed to be used wisely. I had an aggressive goal to raise more capital, so not long after hitting Georgia, I did another "How Can I Be Down" conference. This time, the event was in Atlanta and generated around $70,000. It was everything I needed to feel whole again. I used the money earned from both conferences, along with another $20,000 my dad fronted, and opened Uptown.

The first time I took money from Cynthia was a few months before she moved to Atlanta. She gave me $10,000 and we both agreed it was a contribution to our new life. We thought Uptown would be a dream come true, but it turned out to be a nightmare. When RHOA came about, I knew it could be a catalyst for something greater. Our finances caved in right as we began filming, but we still didn't pour shit over sugar. We never lied, used other people's cars or fronted like we had two or three homes. We just showed what was ours. Even though it was crazy as fuck the first year, I knew *Housewives* would be a means to an end.

When you're young and fall into a hole, you have enough energy and muscle to climb out. When you're older, you're not as fit and energetic to pull yourself up. Cynthia and I used the show to our advantage and made it work for us. I took about 10 percent of our second season earnings to create my next move. Once bar ONE was up and running, my sole focus was to grow our base and make sure we never returned to those rocky waters. I used another portion of the money to teach my wife The Art of the Hustle.

The Bailey Agency did $10,000 in its first month of business, and its overhead was only 20 percent of that. Just a year before, social media haters were telling Cynthia to leave me because I was abusive, broke and angry. It wore her down, but it made me stronger. In June of 2010, I was sitting at home doing nothing. Six months later, bar ONE was poppin' and The Bailey Agency was kicking ass. Cynthia made the right choice in creating a union with me. I didn't feed her fish and rice on a silver platter, but I taught her how to use a fishing pole. If I go tomorrow, she's learned how to go out and sink that line to catch food for herself and Noelle.

As for my future ambitions, I will continue to expand the bar ONE brand. I have aligned with a partner to build two, 3,500-square-foot venues (bar ONE and Sports ONE) in Charlotte, North Carolina. I'm also focusing on getting my piece of the billion-dollar coffee empire, through my newly launched Peter's Brew. A young friend who owns Friday's Coffee, based out of Atlanta, introduced me to a line of Jamaican rum coffee. He saw my personality and West Indian roots as a perfect match and talked me into getting into the business.

I'm even sticking my neck into the awards show arena. Regular, everyday people love reality TV stars, but Hollywood doesn't embrace them. NeNe is one of the few stars to cross over into scripted television. But in today's programming, reality shows are what pay the bills and bring in ratings for a lot of networks. Hollywood finally got the memo that some reality stars are just as big and influential as silver screen celebrities. We have huge social media followings and are seen weekly by millions. The corporate blue suits see us as thieves coming in to steal their jewels. They can't wait for the shit to be over!

Reality television is strong because it costs less to produce and earns more money. It's a no-brainer. Shows like ours had 3.8M viewers in its first run, while HBO's, *Girls* and Martin Scorsese's *Boardwalk Empire* have garnered much less; all at a cost of around two million dollars an episode. I would bet anything that a *Housewives* episode can be produced for a quarter of that cost.

Reality personalities also make a lot of money off camera. They'll take a $10,000 payday to walk through a club or lend their name to an event for $5,000. We draw crowds and increase alcohol sales, because people like our realness and find us approachable. Most actors' pants are too stuck up in their butt cracks to host club gigs.

It's a safe guess to say that none of us will ever get an Emmy or Oscar for our contributions to television. In response, I came up with the idea of *The Unscripted Reality TV Awards*. It will be an invitation-only show, requesting the presence of every reality star on the planet – from *Duck Dynasty* and *Honey Boo Boo* to everybody across the *Housewives* franchise. The first year might be a loss, but it only takes one solid run for every Tom, Dick and Harry to want to jump aboard. No one wants to be on a train that's standing still, but the minute it leaves the station, everybody wishes they would have hopped on.

At our ages, there's not a day that passes that Cynthia and I don't talk about creating financial security for our future. We know that ten years from now, whatever we have, may be *all we will ever have*. So we will continue to stockpile as much as possible with respect to our future. We grind to the point of exhaustion. It's a chance of a lifetime that we both know will come and go quickly. The time is now to do and be all that we ever imagined. When it's all a wrap, nobody will be able to say we didn't beat our hustle to a pulp. Real talk!

CHAPTER VIII
Connecting Flights
Our Blended Family

Peter's Concourse

I T'S INTIMIDATING FOR a woman to hear that a man has multiple kids, so over the years I've developed a super cocky strategy that kills the issue off the top. Whenever I'm asked if I have children, I always respond, "Of course I do! I'm a forty-five-year-old man, why wouldn't I? I have five beautiful kids." The delivery is so arrogant, when women hear it, they can't help but to step up or step off. However, after they learn my five kids are spread over four different mothers, they go in hard like a precinct shakedown for a murder-one charge. I broke it down for Cynthia before she had a chance to put the handcuffs on me.

My two oldest children are products of my first marriage – Porsche is my firstborn, then Peter Jr. My third child is Blaze, Isaiah is the fourth and my youngest is Bryce. Blaze, Isaiah and Bryce have different mothers. When I ran the drill with Cynthia, her facial expression never changed. Her poker face was solid.

Porsche and Peter Jr. came at a time when I was young, dumb and full of it – still trying to figure out my life. I was wild and not the most loyal person. After separating from my first wife, I met Blaze's mom in 1992 and fell for her quick. We had Blaze in '94, and our unfortunate break up happened the following year. I moved back to Miami to open my new restaurant, Savannah, while she and Blaze stayed in New York.

Savannah was an urban hang suite for the *Who's Who* of Miami. Oprah, Stedman and Gayle even spent New Year's Eve one year in our dining room. One of my fondest memories was hosting the Miami Heat's party for one of their conference championship wins. Savannah was known as a South Beach hot spot and a magnet for attracting celebrity beauties. And never being one to take sand to the beach, I was dating a string of starlets and models. I was going through them faster than a roll of single-ply toilet paper.

I had a little girl that I loved and wanted to be there for, but I would have lost so many opportunities being back in New York with Blaze. From the streets to the boardroom – I was making a lot of money in Florida. My success made me obnoxious, and I started feeling myself a little too much. Blaze's mom wanted a stable commitment with me, but my head wasn't in a place to maintain a healthy relationship. Settling down was nowhere in my immediate plans. I was only thinking about myself and couldn't muster the maturity to put my daughter's (or her mother's) needs before my own.

I eventually sold Savannah and left South Beach in 1998 to run the West Coast division of *The Source* magazine. Around the same time, I'd broken up with a Hollywood "it" girl I was dating. I wanted to prove to her and anyone else who doubted me that I could make it out in L.A. I served as executive producer of the most recognized show UPN had ever aired, *The Source Awards*. After I successfully made my mark, I was ready to get the hell out of there. I didn't like the people and couldn't board a damn plane fast enough.

Just before I left L.A., I encouraged Blaze's mom to relocate there. We still were not together, but I maintained constant communication with her since Blaze was my youngest child at the time. California had the contacts she needed to develop a network and market herself as a cinematography agent. I did everything I could do to contribute to her success, and she was open to my input. She turned out to be a little less open to hearing the news that I'd had a one-night stand shortly before her move.

Eight months later, that one night of pleasure called me to say she was about to give birth to a lifetime of reminders. We had slept together, lost contact and I moved back to Miami. We'd never even gone to dinner or a movie! When I got the call, it was mad disturbing. I was riding in a cab with Vivian Scott Chew, answered the phone and the voice on the other side said, "Peter, I'm calling to let you know I'm pregnant." I said, "Congratulations. Who the fuck is this?"

When I realized who she was, I still couldn't understand why she was calling me to announce her pregnancy. I hadn't seen her in almost a year. Then the answer to my question came. She told me the baby was possibly mine. My first thought was that she was trying to hit me up for money. Vivian could hear the conversation and motioned for me to get off the phone. I told her I needed a moment, but I would call her back. Viv asked if I had sex with her. I confirmed that we got busy, but told Viv we had used a condom. At the same time, everything happened on one of those nights I was so wasted, that I would have spelled my first name P.E.T.A.

When I originally met her in California, she'd walked into a room filled with gorgeous people. Even in that crowd, she stood out like a Muslim serving BLTs at the Waffle House. She had a military buzz cut like she was fresh out of the Marines, 5'8", green eyes and olive skin. She was straight butter! I asked her if she was a model and she gave me some sarcastic, feisty answer. I invited her to do a few shots and the next thing I knew, we were at 7-Eleven buying condoms.

I was a player, but a finicky one. My style was to spend time with a woman and get to know her smell before anything happened on a sexual tip. The scent of a woman is critical for me. Even to this day, I'll smell my wife whenever I'm close to her. I love Cynthia's aroma! Sometimes I'll wear her perfume just so I can smell like her all day. When another woman tells me I smell good and asks what I'm wearing I'll tell her, "My wife's perfume, now get the hell on!" It just wasn't my usual thing to sleep with a woman the first time we met. Yet, this one was so milky, I had to drink her. I woke up naked in her bed the next day.

Playing everything back from that morning, I remembered seeing the condom wrapper on the floor, but no condom. My first thought was to look for it. I'd heard some horrible stories about the places missing condoms ended up. Before I could really search for it, I was distracted by her sitting up in bed and lighting a cigarette. I asked her to put it out, and she told me it was her house and I could get the fuck out if I didn't like it. If that was her way of telling me good morning, I figured either she wasn't a morning girl or my sex sucked.

The kind of shit she was kicking me was the very reason that no matter where my night started, it always ended with me sleeping in my own bed. I wasn't a guy who was cool with spending the night at any woman's house. That was some chick shit! There was just something about this girl that had me breaking my own rules left and right. I didn't like nobody putting me out of anywhere, so I honored her request and got to stepping.

Three weeks later, she popped up at my crib. I had no memory of even telling her where I lived. She said she was attending a gay pride parade in the area and asked if she could park her car at my place. We ended up sleeping together again. No tequila shots that time, but I had a tracer on that damn condom we used. I never did figure out what happened to the first one. Fast forward eight months; I'm sitting my black ass in the back of a cab, thinking how all this shit could even be possible.

I had no idea how far along she was and sent her $3,000 for an abortion. The next week, I met her at a restaurant in L.A. and intentionally got there before she did so I could watch her arrive. When I saw her, she was pregnant as shit! I took a paternity test, along with two other guys. My unlucky ass, who had never won anything in my whole damn life, won that time by 99.99999999 percent. I was angry at myself. All of my other kids had been planned. Not only did this birth blindside me, but Isaiah Joseph was my first and only child not to bear my last name.

Cynthia's Concourse

When Peter told me he had five beautiful children, it was still early in the game for us. I didn't feel the need to say anything other than, "that's great" … (for him). I loved that he seemed proud to be a father. Having only one child, I was admittedly curious about how the dynamics worked for Peter, being a dad to so many. I could not imagine his process of coordinating visitation with each of the four moms. Did he visit each child on a rotation system, or did they all just randomly get together, Brady Bunch style?

Two kids would have been more than enough for me, but the second never happened. Having met Peter right before my fortieth birthday, having more children was certainly biologically possible, but not practical. Peter is the kind of guy who wants to procreate with any woman he truly cares about, while I'm fine just *imagining* what the end product would be. Coming to Atlanta, my focus was on solidifying the second half of my career and being the best parent possible to Noelle. A new baby with Peter would have been working backward for me.

I never envisioned myself with a house full of children. I was completely satisfied giving my love and attention to one child. If Peter had no children, I would have certainly been more receptive to giving him one. I don't think I could have denied him the opportunity of becoming a dad. Luckily, he had fatherhood on lock, and we both agreed our soccer team of six was all good.

I made a point of introducing Peter to Noelle *and Leon* early on because I didn't want to get too far down the line and find out they didn't like him. My daughter lived with me. If there were any underlying issues between her and the man I cared about, I needed to know right away. The paradigm was a two-way street between me and Leon. He always made it a priority to introduce me to any woman he was considering bringing around Noelle. I don't think it's good to have your children hanging around people you don't know. I didn't expose Noelle to every man I dated, but once Peter and I started talking marriage, meeting her was the next step in my process.

Once we became an official item, I wanted to meet his kids. I don't remember my introduction to Peter's kids being as vital to him as it was to me. It very much seemed like he was down with me, regardless of how they felt. I, on the other hand, am a big believer that for blended-family marriages to have longevity, a certain harmony has to exist between the kids and stepparents. Lack of harmony does not cancel out the relationship, but it can make things pretty problematic.

He didn't have the Cosby's relationship with his exes that I had with Leon. He couldn't just call them up and say, "Hey, I'm in town. Swing by and meet my supermodel girlfriend!" I stayed completely out of the when, where and how of meeting his exes and kids. If there were any looming disputes that needed to be addressed, it would be Peter's place to resolve them, *not mine*. I had no issue with Peter's number of children, I was merely anxious to get past the formalities

None of the children lived with Peter and were scattered around the country, so I met each indiscriminately. I stayed open and excited, but knew it wasn't my place to interfere with his way of doing things. As long as I felt Peter was making my introduction to each child a priority, I went with the flow and allowed him to control the particulars.

His firstborn, Porsche, was coincidentally the first of his children that I met. It was during the early phase of our dating, while I was still living in New York. Peter had put on an event there and she came to the party. She was charismatic, cute, smart, funny and a quintessential daddy's girl! Her bond with Peter was obviously magnetic. She worked at VH1, had aspirations to become a model and seemed excited to meet me. We were both New Yorkers with a lot in common, which allowed us to develop a closeness outside of Peter. She would come by my place for visits, and I would invite her to attend social outings with me. We grew very friendly and fond of each other.

We would talk about everything, from fashion to man drama. Until the day it hit me that my man was her daddy! Porsche felt she could remain objective, but the reality was we were still venting to each other about the same man. A couple of times, Peter asked me about things that I had only shared with her. Another time or two, I found myself hot with Peter over things Porsche had told me about him. She was getting caught in the middle, and I realized I was putting her in an unfair position. It had never occurred to me that befriending Peter's daughter would become a conflict of interest in being his wife. Things got weird and I knew I had to cut it off.

Porsche was Peter's child and confidante, not mine. Peter deserved the right to talk to her confidentially about anything, even me. I made the decision not to maintain a girlfriend or BFF exchange with her. We ceased all the personal conversation about her dad and established more of a step-mom-stepdaughter connection. My epiphany aided in our relationship eventually growing stronger.

I met Porsche's brother, Peter Jr., next. He was such a handsome, super sweet and talented young man. Peter Jr. struck me as artistically inclined – a little bit of a rapper and musician rolled into one – the caliber of talent that could have a huge music career if he remained focused. His benevolent spirit was a clear indication that he had been raised primarily by a woman. He had so many gentle sensibilities of a momma's boy. My contact with him made me especially curious about the type of woman his mother was. When I finally met her, it was a very pleasant experience. Having only known Peter's perspective of their history, I didn't know what to expect. She made me feel totally welcome and turned out to be approachable and mad cool.

Peter's Airspace

Isaiah had just turned a year old when the paternity test proved he was my son. Blaze's mom and I had already been through so much, I knew if I tried to keep his birth a secret any longer, it would come back to bite me in the ass. She had moved to California to give us another shot, and we'd established a beautiful life and home in Beverly Hills. If nothing else, I owed her the truth. I don't remember her exact response when I came clean, but it wasn't nice! What I do remember is packing my shit and hearing Michael Jackson's "Beat It" playing in the background of my head. She was done with me for good.

It wasn't easy leaving, knowing she had really never done anything foul to me. I wanted to get my act together to be the best man I could for her; we just never got on the same page. I left California around the end of '99 to go back to Miami. Within a two-year period, I opened Barcode Restaurant and Lounge and Static nightclub. I would consistently send funds to support Blaze, and I was also sending money to take care of Isaiah. I did everything in my power to avoid dealing with his mother. Even with the confirmation that he was mine, I spent seven years in denial. It was another not-so-proud period in my life that I wouldn't mind erasing.

My friend Alex Moyer (former NFL, Miami Dolphin player) thought setting me up on a hot date would pull me out of my funk. He wanted to hook me up with a girl I had briefly dated back in '96. In my travels back and forth from Cali to Miami, we had run into each other a few times, so she wasn't completely off my radar. I agreed to go out with her again, and we decided to meet in the lobby of the Tides Hotel. Seeing her again that night, she looked cuter and more settled than when I had last seen her. She was the perfect escape to break the blues after my split with Blaze's mom.

A couple of months later, my homeboy Michael Kyser (current president of Atlantic Records for Black Music) and I held a party for Jay-Z in a suite at the Tides. I had upgraded my pseudo blind date to girlfriend status, and she was there with me. She had a striking beauty that would catch any man's eye, even Jay-Z's. On an elevator ride the three of us shared, we reached our floor and she exited first. As she was walking away, Jay-Z told me, "Man, you gotta hit that." I let him know it was already in the cards. Months later we were living together, and she delivered my youngest child, Bryce Hernandez in 2004.

When we broke up, the experience was the first time I had worn some-one's "Get the Fuck Outta My Life" T-shirt **and it didn't feel too hot**. Her rejection had me experiencing all the pain I had put many of my exes through. I was bitter about it and felt reckless, like I was going to lose it! My mind was playing tricks on me, telling me some foul shit. If you have ever watched an episode of *The First 48*, it doesn't take a brain scan to know the mind can snap quickly. Pain will make you do some shit you'll wind up regretting the rest of your life.

She used Bryce as leverage in our split, and I had to take her to court to get visitation rights to see him. All this went down while I was still trying to stay out the ring with Isaiah's mom. Under the pressure of dealing with both women at once, I was convinced I would never find another woman that I truly loved. The thought of starting a new relationship put a pain in my gut equal to that of a root canal with no Novocain. My negativity hit the brakes the day Melrose reminded me of Cynthia Bailey. Even in our first conversation about buying her truck, I sensed everything about her had the potential to change my life.

In the early months of our dating, I took her to meet my two oldest chil-dren (before any of the others). She and Porsche were in the same industry and shared a love for anything connected to fashion. Porsche had just turned twenty-four and was launching a modeling career in New York. She was beyond excited to meet Cynthia and knew her to be an icon in the modeling world. They hit it off immediately. Watching them relate and listening to Cynthia give Porsche advice made my heart race double time.

Peter Jr. met Cynthia later that same month. He thought she was fine, and she thought he was a good looking, smart kid – *basically, a chip off the old block.* Shortly after meeting Porsche and Peter Jr., Cynthia met Bryce during a trip we took to Miami. It was puppy love at first sight between the two of them.

Where Blaze was concerned, she had never spent time with me and a woman, other than her mom. They still lived out in California, and Blaze wasn't able to meet Cynthia until a year after we started dating. When the day came, Blaze was a little standoffish. I always thought she viewed meeting Cynthia as being disloyal or hurtful to her mom. Cynthia never left home without her big girl panties and perfectly understood Blaze's reserved nature. As with all of my kids, she took absolutely nothing personal when it came to meeting or getting to know her.

It was a relief to get through most of the introductions and give Cynthia a glimpse of how I was as a father. I wanted her to see how much I loved my kids and how much they adored me. My goal was to make her comfortable with my parenting skills, because her daughter would be living with us. Even though Noelle wasn't mine biologically, I still wanted to prove to Cynthia that Noelle would be given the same protection and love that I gave my own children.

By the time Cynthia met my last child, Isaiah, we had been married for a year. Ironically, he has been my only child to live with us. One day, his mom called me out of nowhere to say that he was being disrespectful and acting out. She said his twelve-year-old frame had grown taller than hers and spankings were no longer an effective punishment. She had run out of options and asked if she could send Isaiah to stay with me for a while. When I told Cynthia I needed to take control of the situation, she didn't question my choice for a second. In fact, I think she responded with, "Okay, let's get the guest room fixed up." It only confirmed that I had made the right choice in a wife.

The first time I laid eyes on Isaiah, he was seven years old. I went to California to meet him and his mom on neutral ground at a local park. I remember him saying to me, "You're black!" I told him, "So are you."

Well, he wasn't quite as black as me. He couldn't stop touching my face. I could tell he was happy and already comfortable being around me. I stayed for a week and took him shopping. We spent most of our time talking, with me answering a lot of questions and getting to know him.

His mother was raising him in Big Bear, California, where most of the kids were white. He was a skateboard kid. It tripped me out because in a sense, he was like a white boy with jet black, curly hair – stuffed into black skin. His surroundings led him to question his mom about why he looked so different from his siblings. It made him fretful, and he wanted to see what the other side of his family looked like.

Five years after that initial meeting, Cynthia and I began putting things in place for him to come live with us. When it was time for the move, I sent money to his grandmother to purchase his plane ticket. I didn't send the money to his mom, 'cause I wasn't trying to set it up for her to keep the money and call me talking 'bout she changed her damn mind. When I picked him up from the airport, we went straight to the barbershop and I hooked him up with a fresh haircut. Knowing he already spoke differently from the typical Georgian, I wanted to boost his ego. His surfer-dude look wasn't the hype in the south, so I put him on point with a lil' swag. He saw more black people on his first day in Atlanta, than he had probably seen at a Martin Luther King's Day parade in Big Bear, California.

Cynthia's Airspace

Peter met Isaiah for the first time while we were still dating. His explanation of how Isaiah came into existence is definitely one that can be filed under the classic "The Condom Broke" category. He told me that Isaiah's conception stemmed from a combustible mixture of too much alcohol, raging hormones and sex with a woman he had just met. Not long after the encounter, he relocated to a different city, having no knowledge of her pregnancy. All of the detached elements resulted in him never having a relationship with or getting to know Isaiah's mom. I certainly wasn't going to hire a private investigator to check out his story. Unless I found out otherwise, his rendition was one I could live with. It was part of Peter's past and not something that happened during the span of our relationship. He just got caught out there, and one night became forever.

There was an uncertainty of whether Isaiah would ever come around. I knew from Peter that he had been asking questions about who his father was, so I suggested that Peter make arrangements to meet him. I have always encouraged my husband to accept responsibility for where his choices in life have landed him. I don't have the power to figure out his destiny for him, no more than he can figure out mine for me. I'm just along for the ride as his wife. He handles his part, I handle mine and hopefully somewhere along the journey our purpose will become clearer.

Years after Peter met Isaiah, his mom called to report that Isaiah had started to rebel. I looked at the scenario as if I were in her shoes, and couldn't help but to wonder if it were me, what kind of reaction would I want from the father of my child. I would have desperately wanted my son to be embraced by his dad. It made me proud to know it was exactly how Peter chose to handle the situation. We all agreed it was a good idea for Isaiah to come and spend some time with Peter in Atlanta.

When a custodial parent sends their child to live somewhere else, it's essential for peace of mind to know the child is entering a safe and loving environment. I went out of my way to give Isaiah's mom the same reassurance I would want. Isaiah came to us, identifying more with his white side. He looked black but had a lot of white tendencies. It made sense to me because his mom and siblings were white; he lived in a white neighborhood and had primarily white friends. Atlanta was a culture shock on every level. Collard greens and hot-water cornbread were as foreign to him as his blackness. He liked snowboarding and just about any cold sport you could name – *all of which were not found in the* South. As far as I knew, black people ran from the cold, like it was a form of Kryptonite.

Isaiah was welcomed with outstretched arms into our home. Noelle and I were pretty used to ruling the roost, so adding a twelve-year-old boy to the mix took somewhat of an exorcism. I had to purge all of his boyish habits of eating directly from containers, drinking out of cartons and not washing his hands when he came in from the outside. Noelle was initially excited to have a brother, until her Only Child Syndrome kicked in. All day long she would ask me, "When is he leaving, Mommy?" I had to explain to her that Isaiah wasn't a new toy that she could play with for a few months and toss aside when she got bored.

Other than both having November birthdays, Isaiah and Noelle were very distinct kids. They were from different backgrounds, went to separate schools and their personalities were polar opposites. Every week there was a new battle of the sexes fight to referee. Living with them was like being an extra in a dysfunctional chitlin' circuit play. They would bump heads for days, then all of a sudden, Isaiah would be playing games with Noelle or surfing the net on her iPad. I chalked it all up to just plain, ol' sibling rivalry.

The more Peter stayed out of it all, the smoother the household operated. His over-parenting was completely off the chain! He had a running scroll of pie-in-the-sky mandates for Isaiah. He had to be in bed by eight, eat all his vegetables, brush his teeth after every meal and hang the moon every night before 7:00 p.m. It was ridiculous! Peter's excessive rules created even more discord, and Isaiah started to challenge the variances in the household rules. He wanted to know why Noelle didn't have to go to bed until ten. Why didn't Noelle have to eat all her vegetables? Why didn't Noelle have to do this? Why didn't Noelle have to do that? I allowed everything to run its course, and I remained quiet. As long as it didn't affect my parenting style or Noelle's routines, I supported Peter raising his child as he saw best.

To Peter's credit, Isaiah was adjusting well and showing major signs of improvement. He was happy, his grades were good and he had gained some healthy weight. When he returned home that year to visit him mom during the Christmas break, she liked the child that came back. She had really missed him and ultimately decided Isaiah didn't need to be in Atlanta anymore. It was never her goal to send him to Georgia indefinitely. She was just a mother trying to save her child from himself. She wanted to see a positive change in him, and Isaiah's stay with his father delivered it.

It was interesting getting to know and establish a relationship with Peter's kids. Of them all, Peter's separation from Bryce seemed to cause him the most suffering. There was a stretch of time when Peter didn't see or talk to him for almost a year and a half. His mom had moved on and Bryce had started referring to her new guy as "Dad." It made Peter equal parts furious and sad. Peter's mania naturally played out in our household, and he was consistently a jerk to Noelle and me. He was so hypersensitive to the matter; we had to refer to it as "The Bryce Situation."

I was unsuccessful in comforting him, and it was agonizing to watch the man I loved suffer and not be able to do anything about it. I couldn't wrap my brain around the mindset of a parent who worked so hard to isolate a child from their other parent. I couldn't think of anything that Leon could do to make me keep Noelle away from him. Regardless of how bad things got, I stayed in it with Peter. When he asked, I would advise him on what words or actions I thought a woman would respond to – sometimes it worked, sometimes it didn't. Peter eventually pursued the matter in court until he was finally granted visitation rights.

Not long after getting the order, I went to Miami with Peter to meet Bryce. Peter picked him up and brought him back to our hotel. More than any of his other children, Bryce looked the most like Peter (with fair skin). He was a sweet spirit like his dad, but a boy of few words. I gave him space, didn't make idle conversation or do anything to try and win him over. I simply maintained the role of my husband's advocate. After that visit, Peter began to see him on a regular basis. He also purchased a cell phone for Bryce to call him as often as he wanted.

After an incubation period, Bryce was allowed to come visit us. Based on the selection of clothing and how neatly his things were packed, I could tell his mom was an attentive mother who loved him. He was a well-behaved and uncomplicated child. I was bowled over by his good manners and his need for very little instruction. No matter what it was, he never needed to be told something more than once. When I met his mom, I understood why Bryce was so well-rounded. She was bright, kind and fun. *I was damn near ready to exchange friendship bracelets with her!* Peter swore it wasn't her usual nature, but the woman I met was cool and one I would have enjoyed having cocktails with.

I don't ever try to carry a torch on Peter's behalf or follow the issues he's had with his exes. I see them all as connecting parts of his past that hold five master keys to his future. Kids can't be canceled, and parents have no choice but to work through their differences and be civil. My cardinal rule is to simply listen and stay out of any matters concerning the kids or their moms. My perspective keeps me neutral, worry-free and mess-free.

I'm not looking for a friendship with any of Peter's exes, only an exchange of mutual courtesy and consideration. In my experience with each, I sensed they merely wanted my respect, not necessarily to be liked. They are all rearing great kids and certainly deserve to be revered. It's a small price to pay to any woman raising a man's child as a single parent.

Peter's Direct Flight

Being dropped in Black-lanta was an adjustment for Isaiah...*and Noelle*. She, too, was a multicultural kid who had to get in the rhythm of being around so many blacks when she and her mom moved to Atlanta. Noelle was the princess of the house, and very used to getting everything she wanted. It was almost impossible to get her and Isaiah to share. Noelle's mom sided with her a lot, and it created major conflict between Cynthia and me.

Noelle is the person that Cynthia loves most in the world. She refuses to compromise in any matter involving Noelle. If it comes down to it, she will cut off any man or family member for the sake of her daughter. Cynthia established a clear chain of priorities with me from day one, so

I never tried to play it like I didn't know the deal. In Cynthia's defense, I know she really tried to make the situation with Isaiah work. She cared deeply for him, but at the end of the day, Isaiah wasn't her child. It was just one of those predicaments she didn't see coming. It was difficult for all of us.

I had experienced the same inner battle early on in my relationship with Cynthia. There was a period when I didn't want to be around Noelle. She wasn't my child, and I was missing my own children. On top of my resentment, I kept feeling like Noelle was being instructed not to listen to me. She was smart well beyond her years and knew how to manipulate Cynthia to get her way. Sometimes it felt like I was in a competition with her to see which of us would win Cynthia's approval.

For a long time, I thought it was because Noelle didn't respect me as viable father figure. She never called me "Daddy" or referred to me as her stepdad. I was always just "Peter" to her. In reality, it had more to do with the fact that she already had a bond with her biological father. I still took it personally, because I had been in a similar situation that never required me to jump over as many hurdles.

Bryce's mom had a young daughter who lived with us as well. There were no grandparents to pitch in or help babysit on the fly, because both of my ex's parents were deceased. Not having them around made her appreciative of my involvement in her daughter's life. She would leave her in my care without any hesitation. No matter what anybody else said, did or thought, she always honored my presence and opinions. She had an unwavering trust in my ability to step in as a guardian. It was a totally different experience than the road I traveled with Cynthia and Noelle.

It wasn't that Cynthia didn't trust me with her daughter; she just had a lot of people to answer to. Initially, Leon and Cynthia's mother were opposed to Noelle being left alone with me. Cynthia didn't want any backlash, so she would leave Noelle with the nanny or her mom would come in from Alabama to watch her. It was like their eyes were constantly on me, and they didn't feel she was safe in my presence. It affected me and made me not want to be alone with Noelle until we were all on the same page. I was Cynthia's husband, but the process of getting past all the scrutiny took years.

Just because two people got married, blended families don't blend overnight! The kids have to take their own steps in getting to know one another. Noelle has met all of my children, but she doesn't refer to them as her brothers and sisters – they're *Peter's kids*. Likewise, my children see her as *Cynthia's daughter*. It's a natural, understandable disconnect. They didn't grow up together and they don't live in the same household (or state). Ours is NOT a truly blended family. We are far from *The Brady Bunch*, and Alice ain't in the damn kitchen making oatmeal cookies. True bonds take time and we are all just reaching a place where it's all good.

Noelle now loves me, *and I love her*. Our first three years together were hard. Cynthia played a big role in conditioning her to accept me as a surrogate. Once Noelle began to feel safe, she actually started to miss me when we were away from each other for extended periods. I'd also missed the hell out of her when she was gone. She had a tradition of spending every Christmas in Jamaica with her dad. I knew our relationship had changed when she would return home and my hug would be longer and tighter than the one she gave her mom. I could always tell when she was missing her father too; she would climb into bed with us and lay her head on me with daughterly affection. I love being a dad! Including Noelle, I'm the proud father of six children – three girls and three boys. *If you ask my wife how many kids she has, she'll answer – one.*

Any woman in my life has to be able to accept the baggage that comes along with me. Being responsible for your own luggage is a part of any trip. Even with air travel, you can't just let your bags go before you. They have to travel with you. If you get off, they get off with you. I never lied to Cynthia about all the layers in my life because I wanted to be sure she could accept me for who I was. When you start off with all your skeletons out of the closet, it leaves a lot of room to hang precious memories with someone you really love.

Six years into our relationship, I have absolutely no regrets. I still feel like we were destined to be together. People can't fathom seeing me without Cynthia or her without me. We were introduced to America as a couple, and it's why millions continue to watch us weekly. If we're not together five years from now, I know people will still be asking me, "Where Cynthia at?" So, I might as well stay with her ass and make it pop! The process of becoming one has been fucked up with all types of potholes, but we manage to stay on course because we believe there's something better ahead.

Every day, we continue to work through the details. A lot of relationships can't survive an ex-spouse and one kid. Cynthia and I are thriving, with a prized collection of six kids, four baby mamas and one baby daddy. We maintain open communication about everything. We are honest about who we are, where we've been and where we're going.

Cynthia's Direct Flight

With certain children, Peter is very firm, but he's a lot more delicate and tiptoes around matters with Blaze. Of his children, I met her last. By the time it happened, I was aggravated and leery of why Peter kept postponing our introduction. I reached a point where I stop asking when or if it would ever happen. He didn't push for it the way he did with his other children. There was definitely something shady about the delay, but I couldn't put my finger on it.

Peter was so closed and treated that part of his life like an untouchable X-file (or *ex-file* I should say). He didn't talk about it and rarely answered my questions. From the way he spoke of Blaze's mom, she was someone he would have eventually married. A part of me wondered if they were still kicking it on the side. Peter and I would visit L.A. frequently, but he never offered to introduce me to Blaze's mom. To this day, she is the only ex that I have never met.

I had consistently put all my cards on the table, and it bothered me that Peter seemed to be holding back. I wanted full access to all parts of his life – or at least equal to what I had given him. After two whole years, I finally met Blaze. She was very polite and very "Team Mom." I allowed her to tell me what she wanted and let the conversation unfold naturally. I don't liked being pushed, so I'm not in the business of prodding others to do anything that doesn't come naturally.

I could see that Blaze's mom had a shroud of protection around her by the number of times she called and the manner in which Blaze answered our questions. I wasn't tripping, because I was guilty of the same inquiring behavior with Noelle. I treated my first meeting with Blaze as I'd done in my initial one with Bryce. I gave her space, did more listening than talking and didn't try to become stepmother of the year in our first encounter.

After our trip to L.A., Blaze came to Atlanta and stayed with us for a week. She and Noelle got along well. I wanted her to grow comfortable organically in our home and around me. I work with people's energy and what their body language tells me, so I only talked when she wanted, went along on errands if she asked and didn't push. I wasn't around her a lot during her stay, but in the time we spent together, I found her to be very smart and polite. I understood and respected her loyalty to her mom.

Her mom was her rock, and without having met her, I could confidently compare my style of mothering to Blaze's mom. My degree of protection over Noelle seemed overbearing to Peter, so I would liken my style of parenting to Blaze's mom to help him identify with why I was so guarded when it came to Noelle. Similar to Blaze and her mother, Noelle was my only daughter and child. As mothers, I believe we both took a certain amount of pride in being a constant and dependable support system for our children.

I go to great lengths to avail myself to Noelle. I accept complete liability for her life and her well-being. When Peter and I met, she was eight years old. She had a dad who was highly visible in her life, so I wasn't looking for a father for Noelle. I was seeking a companion for myself. Other than loving her and being there when she needed him, I had no fatherly expectations of Peter. I have never asked him to take an active role in rearing her. Men like to feel needed, so I always knew he would rather be involved than not.

At times I think he resented not having a bigger part in her parenting. In the same vein, I felt he was relieved to have a pass because of all the other duties he had to juggle. Between running several businesses, traveling and fathering – Peter's cup was already running over. Noelle didn't need to be another variable in his problems. I didn't want to overwhelm him with any more stress than he already had. Although I welcomed it, it was not Peter's responsibility to play a part in my daughter's upbringing.

Before we married, we discussed whether Noelle would call him Peter or something else. We agreed that using his first name was the best option. Both of my parents remarried after their divorce, but I only referred to my biological parents as "Mom and Dad." I raised Noelle the same way. The thought of her calling Peter "Dad" was weird and off-putting to me. She had a dad who was alive and well. She didn't need the unnecessary confusion.

Noelle is fortunate because she gets the benefit of having two very different, but strong father figures in her life. Leon is a communicator who is very calm and Zen, while Peter is more cut and dry. Since they are total opposites, there are certain things Noelle will go to Peter about and things she will discuss only with her dad.

Peter and Noelle have an unspoken bond, and I'm amazed at how well she reads his energy. On a day when he's funny and in a good place, she will invite him out to a movie. When he's having an Oscar the Grouch moment, she will just opt to hang out with her friends. She loves distance and being in the solitude of her own space. In that sense, she and Peter are very much alike.

Knowing that Noelle enjoyed spending time alone and being in her own world, I allowed her to befriend Peter's kids in the same laid-back manner that I had. Noelle was mainly concerned with her own interests, but I knew it had to cross her mind how Peter's kids would affect her life. Titles have a way of making things messy, so I never shoved the notion down her throat that his children would be her new brothers and sisters. She naturally took to each of them without any urging.

Peter's kids are amazing and I've never witnessed them be anything less than well-mannered and considerate. They each have unique personalities, but when they're all in a room together, it works. There is never any pressure for anyone to be anything other than who they are. Peter definitely goes into Papa Smurf mode when they're around. He gets a kick out of being the dominant, authoritative figure. My main goal is to keep the house clean and all the mouths fed. I'm the kind of mom who wants to make sure everybody has everything they need.

Regardless of what Peter has told me about his exes, I know that boundaries and mutual respect have to be present for blended families to coexist. The adults sometimes get caught up in the afflictions of their history, instead of the welfare of the children. I never allowed Peter to make things about his exes *or* me. My concern was always centered on what was best for all of our children. It's a simpler way of dealing with a situation that, under normal circumstances, would be painfully complicated. Overthinking and pointless emotion is what makes it complex.

It only takes one glance at Peter's children to know they have been cherished, loved and cared for with all the love a mom could give. Their mothers have done sensational jobs in producing fine human beings. I have always given Peter just as much credit, because I know raising good kids requires a great deal of work from both parents. I'm impressed by his choice of such solid, upstanding women to mother his children. In the end, Peter's circumstances are no different than my situation with Leon. As a couple, we didn't work, but we stayed committed to raising a balanced and happy child. Peter and his exes are cut from the same fabric. We all understand that relationships come and go, but the kids created in them are forever.

CHAPTER IX

Mile-High Club
Our Intimacy

Peter's Bumping

L IKE MOST RELATIONSHIPS in the beginning, Cynthia and I had an explosive sexual and physical attraction. Every time we saw each other we would jump right into it. The sex was always incredible! It was all we wanted to do. Once she moved to Georgia and we set up shop, our frequency stopped like school lunches during Christmas break. We went from several times a week, to a few times a month – *down to once every full moon*. The stress of our finances and the show put a huge dent in our intimacy.

Going into our fourth season on the show, you would think we'd have more bedroom time and be beyond caring what people think of us. It's the exact opposite. Cynthia is still stalking the hell out of Twitter and social media! She has an insatiable need to keep up with everything that's posted, tweeted, liked or mentioned about us. It works for her in some strange way, but it pisses me off in every way. She's still stuck in her morning and nightly routine of checking the latest Peter and Cynthia dish. It's like she's having an online affair right in my face. Most nights, I just go to sleep and dream about all the things I could be doing to her.

On a good day, when she's feeling frisky, she'll put down the iPad and come to bed wearing a T-shirt and no panties. I'll know for sure that she's in the mood when she positions herself seductively in the middle of our bed, instead of lying on her side. Sometimes, she'll just reach over and start sensually caressing my hand. It's like she saying, *"I'm throwing you a bone, Negro...throw me ONE back!"*

She knows it's always about her scent for me. I'll enjoy the foreplay of her touch for as long as I can take it, but when I lean over and smell her... it's on! That's around the time she'll tell me to get up and lock our door. We learned the hard way that you don't have sex behind an unlocked door, with an adolescent in the house.

If ever Noelle would call out a few times to Cynthia and not get an answer back, she would come to the bedroom door and try the knob. Before I came along, Noelle was an only child living alone with her mom, so I understood the habit. Now, we make sure the damn door is locked before the clothes come off! Whenever my wife walks in and locks the doors behind her right away, I already know it's gonna be one of those *don't come knocking if the door frame is rocking* kind of nights.

The better her workday goes, the greater my chances of scoring between the sheets. Still, we don't have time for it the way we used to. Cynthia and I are at a stage where we're doing everything possible to never be financially screwed again. When you've suffered through all that we have, unless you're sitting on a stack in the bank, you become preoccupied with getting your money up. We don't have an obsession with it, but there's an awareness that it could all be gone again tomorrow.

I'm not saying I don't think about sex. The thought pops in my head ten times a day, every day! When I see Cynthia stepping out of the shower or getting dressed, my mind naturally goes there. She is sexy, intricately built and fine as hell. I know there's a long line of men on hold, hoping our shit won't work out, but I don't entertain the ratchetness. I'm too focused on trying to get with Cynthia whenever and wherever I can. Just the thought of her makes me want to get up in the morning and work my ass off. She motivates me to go the distance at a pace that's unheard of.

We're on a mission to get more bar ONE franchises established and The Bailey Agency on concrete ground. Fortunately, our opportunities take us on the road pretty frequently, and we are able to use the time to reconnect as a couple. Once, we were in Los Angeles on business and got back to our room around seven in the evening. It was a no-brainer moment. No kids, a beautiful suite, sturdy mattress and nothing but time on our hands. Cynthia looked at me and asked, "Baby, you wanna have sex?" I was like, "Really? Hell yeah!"

Cynthia beyond satisfies me, and I'm a brutha who always completes any assignment I'm given in the bedroom. Getting away from our everyday surroundings has a way of putting us back into the mix. My thing is taking Cynthia to a tropical paradise a couple of times a year. We were intimate as hell during the time we spent in Anguilla for the renewal of our wedding vows. Dropping us in a striking setting is like putting a new pack of batteries in our back. We work hard at finding "us time," but we understand that a successful relationship isn't just about good sex; it's also about power and access.

Ten years from now, we don't want to be in a situation where we're lacking for anything. Noelle will be in college and my youngest will be on his way. We're setting up to coast through the second half of our lives and generate the financial freedom to truly enjoy each other. I just pray we will have the physical stamina and good looks we have today. It would be a shame to have a shit load of money and not be attracted to each other – or be too broke down to spend it.

We want to tap into a level of security where we're able to maintain our independence well past our seventies. The last thing we want is to have to rely on handouts from others. With age, it's normal for parents to depend on their kids for support, but it's a burden we don't want to put on them. We are parents who take an extreme amount of satisfaction in supporting our children. I want us to be the kind of support system that my dad was for me. When I needed him most, he didn't blink an eye at giving me every dime he could put his hands on to build Uptown. I was at an age when I should have been setting up my parents for their future, but they were still reaching back to help me. Cynthia and I are creating the groundwork for prosperity that will not only take care of us, but also our parents and children.

Cynthia's Bumping

Sex is a priority in the beginning of any relationship. It's a time where everything is new, fun and both people are still exploring each other. New couples have *tired sex* when they're busy. *Regardless of the place or time, they get it in.* As a relationship grows, tired people take their asses to sleep! If given the choice between eight hours of sleep or having sex, I'm going for the eight hours. Peter and I are sexually matched, but his bark is so much bigger than his bite that he would never admit it. When he says he could have sex every day, in his mind he's really just projecting a Cinemax After Dark fantasy. In real life, he works extremely hard and needs sleep at the end of a long day. We are both happiest after a full night's rest.

I have been a career woman my whole life. If I were a stay-at-home mom, I'd probably have the energy to be more domestically diverse. It's hard being Superwoman – a mother, lover, wife and entrepreneur. It's an unrealistic goal to think any woman can wear all those hats and still make sex a daily priority. As his wife, I realize I have a responsibility to take care of Peter's needs. But as an equal-parts contributor to our household, I don't feel it's fair for him to expect sex as often as he would if I didn't work. Between the responsibilities of my agency, appearances, travel and household demands – I do good just to take off my full face of Broadway makeup at night.

I know Peter wants sex on a more consistent basis, and sometimes he'll even get a little pouty about not getting it. Especially if I've worn some-thing sexy that got his blood pumping. He's a man that wants what he wants, when he wants it. I could have on a freshly steamed dress, ready to walk out the door and he'll be trying to crack the code on my zipper.

I strive to give him quality time at least once a week. Personally, I would be good with a delicious meal and a glass of wine. I just like spending time with my husband. However, I take that extra step and try to make our date night a little more special with a romantic dinner and movie. If one of us isn't already snoring by the time the candles are lit, I'll even throw in some sex.

I'm not asserting that a working woman should have a permission slip to deprive her man, but I do feel honesty and setting realistic expectations goes a long way. Even if I'm too tired or too busy to give up the goodies, I will at least acknowledge Peter and give him a specific time when we can be together. He's usually good with that. In the absence of sex, the bedroom connection is still important. At minimum, Peter can always expect cuddling and my leg kicked over his. My foot has to be rubbing his leg in order for me to fall asleep. Once I feel his skin next to mine, all is right in my world.

Sexual compatibility is an important denominator in choosing a mate. I'm more concerned with quality than quantity. I'd rather have great sex twice a month than okay sex every day. In my twenties, my perspective was a lot different. I would have had sex on a private jet at twenty-six, but I'm too much of a germaphobe at forty-six. Peter and I aren't spring chickens. We're both approaching fifty, and at our ages, pulling over on the highway to have sex sounds more dangerous than erotic. That's some old freaks out there doing all that creative screwing. *Consistent sex is freaky for us.*

We have our own unspoken language of intimacy. Peter can pick up on my body energy when I'm giving him the green light for action. If I move to the center of our bed, that's his hint to pass into the red-light district. He also knows when there's a chance for him to score, simply by the way I position myself in bed. But if I'm lying with my pillow fluffed up just right, in a perfectly cozy spot – *ain't no magic happening unless David Copperfield is hiding under the bed.*

When the time does come, there is nothing lacking in our lovemaking. On a scale of one to ten, I would say my freak number is right in the middle at five, a respectable eight! Peter is definitely a great, attentive lover. Somebody lied if they ever said Peter Thomas didn't know how to do the damn thang! When we get down, *we get down!* Peter knows my one-day sales aren't very frequent, so when the Cynthia Bailey store is open for business, he always tries to get a little of everything.

We are so busy trying to revive our fortune that intimacy has taken on a different meaning. We've learned there are so many ways to express tenderness in a marriage outside of sex – from holding hands to watching a movie and eating popcorn in bed. Sex is important for us, but not all the time. It's not a sign of a trouble in our marriage, it's maturity. Being two very passionate and driven people, we find intimacy in supporting each other's careers.

I love to see Peter in a suit, being a boss, telling people what to do. Success is sexy. Power has always been a major turn-on for me. It makes us desirable to each other. Our marriage may seem like a business to some, but when you start out a relationship in the red, it's a nonstop quest to get in the black. Once we achieve a certain level of success, we'll be able to enjoy each other without having fears of the unknown.

Different things work for different couples. A woman who can talk goals and business strategies will get my husband harder than Mount Rushmore. Peter and I have experienced sex from the rags and the riches sides of the bed. I can say firsthand that *successful sex is a lot more fun than broke sex.* Financial freedom is more captivating than any piece of lingerie in Frederick's of Hollywood. When your money is funny and Comcast has blacked out all but three channels, sex doesn't come up a lot. The hot topic of the day is usually centered on how to get the damn cable back on.

Peter doesn't share that disposition. Our mortgage company could be auctioning off our property, while Georgia Power is out back shutting off the meter, and Peter would still be trying to squeeze in a ten-minute quickie. *Where the hell they roll like that?* Sex is mental for me! I have to be completely at peace. If I'm happy, *I'm more than happy to have sex.* If I'm not relaxed mentally, there is no way my body can get into it. I operate primarily off how I feel, and my moods definitely dictate my sexual habits.

I'm the best lover when I'm centered. On our vacation to Anguilla, where Peter arranged for our vow renewal, I was in such a beautiful space emotionally. Noelle was being cared for by my mom, and there was lots of good food and wine. Peter and I were both calm. I was happy to give him a piece every day – sometimes twice a day. When we have those moments, it reminds us both of how great we are when we're well-balanced.

In relationships, the goal is to relish as many extraordinary moments as possible. Peter and I are authentic enough to own who we are and all our differences. We are happily married, attracted to each other and realistic about our sexual capabilities. There is no one formula that works for all couples. Every marriage has bad times; that's why it's important to enjoy the hell out of the good ones. We have those sweet and bitter intervals, just like any other normal couple. Some months are great and everything falls into place – where all the kids are happy, everyone makes honor roll and nobody asks for any money. But we also have months where Murphy's Law wreaks havoc on our household. Both of us are imperfect, so the expectation for the relationship to be perfect doesn't exist.

Peter's Flotation Device

The way we express intimacy progresses as our relationship does. I get off on Cynthia just putting her legs over mine at night or watching her get dressed. I look at her and think, *"Yeah, all that's mine."* By the same token, being married to a woman like Cynthia comes with the pressure of keeping my ass in the gym. I want her flame to always be lit for me! She makes it clear that I satisfy her, but it's not enough for me. I want her to roll over in the morning, look at me and want to eat my ass alive. If I had it my way, she'd be trying to give me *some* every time she sees me. I want to be her eye candy, and keep it together for her the way she does for me. Even the thought of her not being attracted to me anymore makes me want to drop down and do a hundred push-ups.

The whole keeping it sexy thing is for my benefit too. I don't want to just look good in my clothes – *I want to look great.* I'm not trying to be the sixty-year-old guy in the back of the bar with the potbelly. I want to be able to look down over my belt and see my shit. *It's not a good look to have to stand in front of a mirror to find your family jewels.*

My dad is seventy-five years old, and for a dude who's had a quadruple bypass, he looks remarkable. He's a Jehovah's Witness that gets plenty of stares from the ladies when he walks into the Kingdom Hall for Sunday service. I know my mom gets a kick out of it and is more than proud to be on his arm. When I'm seventy-five, I want Cynthia to have that same reaction to me.

I look at intimacy in a relationship like a pilot light; sometimes you turn it up and let it rip – sometimes you turn it down and let it simmer. We're not pups in our thirties, we're old dogs. We are in a period of extreme grind that keeps us exhausted, so we look for ways to be intimate without sex. Working with the one you love to build an empire is stimulating. We're naturally competitive and absolutely refuse to settle for anything less than what we're shooting for. I can't think of a greater intimacy than having a mission shared by a couple. We appreciate every moment together.

We challenge each other on every level. I love teaching her things, but because she's so introspective, I've probably learned a lot more from her. I want it all and see everything as a business, while Cynthia puts things into true perspective, helping us stay grounded. Her strong standards help me set boundaries, specifically in business. For example, once I'm home, there are very few matters that can't wait until morning to be handled. So, I now instruct my staff not to call me between 10:00 p.m. and 10:00 a.m.

I've gotten better at managing my work balance and outside distractions. Women approach me with jump-off angles on a daily basis, but I don't see or think about any woman but my wife. Only one in a thousand will come at me crazy and say something fucked up. Most make it clear that they want us to win, and tell me how much Cynthia and I inspire them. We love it. It makes us want to fight harder for each other and find happiness in our marriage. We never stop thanking God his many miracles and blessings.

Cynthia's Flotation Device

It turns me on to know I do it for Peter. Since day one, he's looked at me like a plate of smothered pork chops with a side of candied yams. I find it alluring he is so attracted to me that he can't hide it. He is committed in a way that doesn't require a fidelity chaperone. Not even for a second have I given pause to the possibility of Peter having a sexual relationship with another woman. I'm not saying he won't flirt, but I can't see him going Monica Lewinsky.

As a bar owner, his business is entrenched in the nightlife. Whodini said it best when they put it on blast that "the freaks come out at night." Certain women aren't deterred by a man wearing a band on his ring finger. I always remind Peter that a woman who would sleep with a married man is also one who would be sure to tell the world about it. That is especially true if that man is on a hit reality show and goes by the name of Peter Thomas. I go to sleep at night with the assurance that Peter fully knows how much he has to lose. He understands that stepping outside of our marriage would be a game changer.

In my mind, infidelity is usually a sign of some type of emotional or spiritual tear in a relationship. I can't unequivocally say that I would leave him if he cheated. We've had a lot of ups and downs, but made it through. Depending on the details, length of the encounter and whom it was with, I might deem it a forgivable act. I would even be a big enough woman to agree to a temporary separation if I felt it would help repair our marriage.

It is very apparent to me when Peter is unhappy in our relationship. When he enters a dark place, there are a lot of indicators that scream out to me. In those moments, I can honestly say it would not surprise me if he strayed. Now if things between us were in a sweet spot and he cheated, I would be completely thrown off. That would seem reckless and most definitely be grounds for the locks to be changed.

I don't think that fulfilled partners in healthy relationships cheat. The reason an outsider is able to connect with a married man is because he, or his marriage, is fragmented in some way. I'm not talking about a man who is a straight-up ho or has a sexual addiction. I'm speaking of a normal, decent, everyday Joe Schmo who loves his wife and family. In a light, beautiful place, that man would probably never cheat for the sake of extracurricular sex. Cheating isn't just about sex. I think it has more to do with seeking out some type of companionship. A lot of men won't cop to that being the case, maybe thinking the truth will only hurt their spouse further.

It's fair to say that the weight of infidelity in a marriage is often shared by both spouses. Obviously, the faithful spouse doesn't hold the same level of blame as the one who actually committed adultery. But there is usually some emotional breech both partners are equally accountable for. Not stopping the bleeding can be just as bad as inflicting the wound.

Checking in with your partner and staying emotionally attached is a never-ending job. Sometimes when Peter travels, I'll put a card or sweet note in his suitcase to let him know how much I love him. When he's away for long spells, we'll keep it hot with some spicy phone sex. I like being creative and coming up with romantic ideas to keep our fire lit. Peter knows my schedule is just as hectic as his, so he gives me credit for the time I work outside of our home. He acknowledges any attempt I make at being one with him. I'm glad to know I can satisfy my man with a tin can of Mrs. Fields cookies instead of having to bake Grandma's homemade recipe.

We love giving gifts that the other truly wants and desires, rather than trying to force our personal likes on each another. I'm very practical and would prefer a spa gift certificate over candy, flowers and a teddy bear. We like picking things out for ourselves or receiving an envelope of money to spend however we choose. It was a bit of a process to get Peter to understand, but he now respects that I am vocal and specific about what I like. As a husband, it makes his job much easier. Real love gives a woman the confidence to be honest with her man about what she wants. At our age, we know honesty is a gift to a marriage.

We are only as great as the best relationships we've had. A man's creativity is often limited by his previous mate's likes and dislikes. Men are prone to carrying over behaviors and habits that satisfied their last lover. Their brain automatically thinks that what worked for one should work for another, not realizing how incredibly different two women can be. If a man is convinced that flowers and chocolate are a romantic gift, but his woman is allergic to flowers and hates chocolate, his strategy is flawed.

I love being able to own who I really am and only give what I'm capable of extending in a relationship. I'm easily turned off by a man who doesn't get me or has it in his head that he can lure me into doing one of his hobbies that I dislike, *like fly fishing and shit.* My maternal grandmother died at ninety-eight. She earned the right to say and do whatever she wanted. It was liberating to watch her not apologize for her positions on things. The golden years are when you know yourself and stop caring about what people think of you. It feels wonderful to say, "I don't want to kiss you right now because your breath stinks," and not have to defend it.

Sexual communication is important. It's all about energy and Peter and I have great chemistry together. We have a mature intimacy, and our lovemaking is a special bond that helps us to continually appreciate one another. Peter knows if he comes home and a candle is burning, he's about to strike gold. But if the long johns are on and my weave is already wrapped, he knows it's just that…*a wrap! And he better not wake me for nothing!*

CHAPTER X
Prepare for Landing
Our Next Chapter

Cynthia's Direct Flight

I SAW MY TRANSITION to Atlanta as an opportunity to remove myself from the public eye, but the complete opposite happened. I stepped out of the limelight, right smack into a bright spotlight. What awaited me in Georgia was bigger than anything I had ever experienced in New York. People in the fashion and beauty business knew of me, but at best, I was only recognizable. Outside of the industry, people didn't know me well enough to put my name with my face. Starring in one of the highest-rated reality shows, millions of people became acquainted with both.

One of the quotes I live by is, "We have our plan, and God has His." Looking back on all the rapid change that ripped through my life in a span of three years, I learned God also has a wonderful sense of humor. I was looking forward to slowing down and gaining more balance, especially in the romance department. I'd obviously had my share of failed relationships – from the wrong man at the right time – to right man at the wrong time. With Peter, knowing all the planets aligned gave me such a sense of anticipation. Little did I know, the universe had an entirely different strategy in motion.

RHOA created a kind of instant stardom that I didn't know existed outside of Hollywood. As a model, my fame matched my work and exposure, but as a reality star I was more famous than my two *Essence* magazine covers. Nothing I had ever done could have prepared me for it. I literally walked into Kroger one day and the whole checkout lane was like, "There's Cynthia Bailey!" It was astonishing to realize I could achieve that level of recognition just from sharing the inner workings of my life on television.

The *Housewives* machine gave me a voice to speak, promote and inspire people in any manner I chose. It was an overwhelmingly powerful privilege that I never had in my previous line of work. Still, I struggled with putting my whole life on display and having so much of my independence revoked. All the attention brought on by the show required me to alter my independence.

I miss the days of doing the majority of my own shopping and buying Noelle's school supplies. For the most part, I now mostly have to send assistants to do simple errands that I'd prefer doing myself. Some days I just want to turn it all off for a few hours to go to the grocery store or pick up the dry cleaning without taking pictures with someone. There is no off switch! I always have to be on and in a full-beat face of makeup, rather than just kicking it in a pair of sweats.

For whatever reason, Walmart shoppers are huge *Real Housewives* fans. During a quick toiletry run, the chance of a person approaching me is more than probable. It only takes one before everybody in the damn feminine care aisle has clocked me. I'm the master of disguises, but my voice is always a dead giveaway. I'll be on the phone and someone will walk up to me like a long-lost cousin and ask, "Cynthia? Girl, is that you?" And they don't just want to take a picture and leave, *they want to engage*! It's not uncommon to hear, "Wait a minute. Hold up and let me call ma dear so you can say hey." Then mama gets on the phone and starts instructing me to tell Kandi to stop selling sex toys. All I can say is, "Okay, alright. Yes, ma'am. You take care now!"

On the show, Peter and I are not portraying fictionalized characters. People see our real lives, and those who have watched from the beginning feel they are a part of our family. They have sat down at our kitchen table for dinner, attended our wedding at the Fernbank and our vow renewal in Anguilla. They have access to us that they would never have to A-list celebrities like Angelina Jolie and Brad Pitt.

It's such a sudden shift in my life that even today I often forget I'm on television every week. Seeing people whispering and pointing is always my wake-up call. Once, on a trip to New York, I couldn't get a cab and jumped on a train to Eighty-Third Street. It was not until people began staring and hissing that I asked myself, "*Why the hell did Cynthia of The Real Housewives hop her ass on this train?*" It's quite an interesting juggling act between the real world and my television world. The true reality check was a night I was out alone, pumping gas, when two men approached me. It scared the living shit out of me.

Peter now fills up my car and insists that I have someone with me at all times, especially when I travel. His solution is not a realistic fix, because I enjoy and desperately need solitude. Occasionally, I'll just want to sit by myself and have a quick burrito in a corner booth of a restaurant. I refuse to have handlers or "security" as Kenya would call them. Traveling with an entourage has never been my thang, but I'm still working on protecting my private space as effortlessly as some of my cast mates.

My fellow housewives have mastered strategies for getting through everyday, public situations. When flying commercial, some will pay a vehicle to take them straight to the tarmac, where they can walk right onto the plane. NeNe and I still prefer the old-fashioned way. When NeNe is in travel mode, she doesn't play. She's amazing at saying no to people when it infringes on her space or time. She won't hesitate to say, "Thank you for watching the show, but I cannot take a picture with you right now. I'm trying to catch the same plane you're boarding." Meanwhile, my ass is still stuck down at security – signing autographs and taking pictures.

It's weird having so much attention for just being me. I'm still learning how to be famous. After the last reunion show, I was looking forward to *The Real Housewives of Beverly Hills* coming up in rotation. It was really naïve to think it would allow me a few months of peace and anonymity. *Every day is a reminder that the influence of the beast never ceases.* All of it has made me more compassionate, and I certainly identify with celebrities who go into hiding and shut themselves away.

Years ago, I remember hearing that Mariah Carey had checked herself into a facility to recuperate from exhaustion. When I heard the report I thought, *"Why the hell can't she just take some time off and go her ass to sleep?"* Now I understand! Public people have to find a way to maintain their sanity and keep a part of their lives sacred. It's also the explanation for why I live in the heart of Atlanta, but never see hometown celebs like Tyler Perry or Usher in public. They would probably get mobbed if they stepped foot into a grocery store or an airport security checkpoint.

I just have too much respect for people's privacy to interrupt. God forbid my biggest photo-op fantasy, Oprah Winfrey, would ever walk into the same room with me. It probably would be a missed opportunity of a lifetime. Though I have never been the kind to approach a celebrity, I have always been very judgmental toward those who turn their fans away. I could never understand why the hell stars wouldn't just take a quick picture or scribble their name on a damn napkin. I thought the whole notion of one person asking another for an autograph was cool. These days, I think it's cool to sit down, have dinner and actually eat my food while it's hot.

The one place where I have indisputably always stood my ground is when I'm out with Noelle. I have a zero-tolerance policy when she is with me. She has told me on several occasions that she would rather stay home than have me be in *"Housewives* mode" during our outings. She doesn't like being approached and sees it as an invasion of her privacy. I still take the time to thank fans for their support, but explain that I'm spending time with my daughter and cannot interact. If we are somewhere having dinner, I'll offer to chat or take a picture before we leave.

My time with Noelle has become more about quality than quantity, and she takes every moment with me very seriously. Prior to being on the show, I always had availability to focus on her and everything she took an interest in. Now, I miss a lot because I'm always working and traveling. I can't recall the last time I sat down and checked her homework. The demands of my career require me to do more parenting from afar and be less hands-on.

I try to explain to Noelle that the window to maximize my exposure is very limited. Everything that I do is ultimately for the betterment of her future. I used to feel terrible about it until I realized I have no greater priority than taking care of myself and my family. My work allows me to pay for Noelle's pricey private schooling and creates more options for her choice of colleges. The downside is that she has to be more independent to give me the space to work.

Going out in public with Peter has taken on a whole new look as well. In a sense, we have replaced our real selves with the RHOA images that the public expects to see. Unlike me, Peter is out there in the thick of it every day. He doesn't have a choice, because he has a small staff and tons of obligations. He enjoys doing his own runs to the bank and farmers' market, but Peter is not the kind of guy you wanna just roll up on. His body language and energy shout, *"Proceed with caution!"* It takes a special kind of fan to approach him.

Our first two years together were fairly normal. We would sit in a reasonably-priced restaurant, clean our plates and lick our fingers at the end of our meal. After four years as a visible reality couple, our date nights are mostly confined to some overpriced, mediocre place that's up in the cut. The clientele in higher-end restaurants recognize us, but usually allow us to enjoy dinner and be left alone. Given the choice, our preference for a meal would be somewhere like The Cheesecake Factory or Sunday brunch at Copeland's, but the meal would quickly turn into an Instagram shoot or a three-hour meet and greet.

In the end, we are nothing without our fans and those who have followed us season after season. We feel blessed beyond expression that people even give a damn whether bar ONE is successful, The Bailey Agency flourishes or we continue on the show. Losing a share of our privacy pales in comparison to all the love and support we get back. We take people's curiosity with a grain of salt, knowing that their interest is what truly makes us relevant. At the end of the day, our fans have become extended family members and we wouldn't have it any other way!

Peter's Direct Flight

Growing up, my parents hid a lot of issues that existed in their marriage. As a kid you don't understand it, but with age your gut becomes stronger and you start to question stuff. In my youth, people always went out of their way to tell me I would grow up to be just like my father. I never took it as a compliment because I didn't want to be what I saw in him. I never wanted to have dreams and not see them fulfilled.

I didn't want to follow in my mother's footsteps either. I could not stomach the thought of settling or missing out on all the possibilities life had in store for me. That's not a hit against my parents; witnessing their struggles firsthand just taught me to aim bigger. The resources they had in their time were far less than what I was blessed to work with in mine. I can only love and honor them for all the sacrifices they made.

When I met Cynthia, I was determined to establish something with her that I'd never had or seen. I knew I couldn't hold the number-one slot, because it was already taken by her child. Being a man who can deal with honesty, I chose to roll with it. I loved Cynthia enough to be number two, *not for another man,* but for her daughter. Second base was never a good look for me until the day Noelle's dad showed me it could be a position of strength, depending on how it was played.

Before we tied the knot, Cynthia decided to have a breast job. Leon came to the hospital the day of her surgery. I was shocked to see him. It messed me up when he told me he was just there to have my back and make sure Cynthia came through safely. This was a man standing in the gap for my woman, even though he had been out of the picture for years.

It wasn't like he would get a chance to see or even test drive the new product. He was just there for support, no strings attached. From that day, I knew Leon loved and cared about Cynthia in a way that was unshakeable. It didn't have shit to do with whether they were together or not. It was more about him being a man of rock-solid values. I will always have the utmost respect and admiration for that brutha.

That involvement with Leon schooled me, and helped me see that there's a teachable moment in every relationship, if you're open to learn. It's delusional to go into a marriage thinking it's going to be all strawberries and cheesecake. In order for a marriage to have a fair shot, it has to start off with both people being hopelessly in love with each another.

Both partners have to be open to working around the other's weaknesses, and both should know each other well enough to predict the other's response in the most heated battle. Cynthia and I were together a couple of years before getting hitched. It gave me the chance to see her at her best and her worst. I had an idea of what would put her over the edge and what would send her packing. She wasn't able to bounce back as quickly as I could, which meant I would usually be the sponge to absorb all the hardship.

That's why spirituality is a huge element in a marriage. It gives any couple greater odds of making it. If God isn't first, even the simplest things are hard to jump off. Cynthia and I were not as focused on our spiritual growth before becoming a couple. We had accumulated a lifetime of experiences between the two of us, but instead of making us bigger, it made us smaller. We were combative and struggled to merge our outlooks on how a couple should come together. I think premarital counseling would have forced us to confront the root of our issues.

We were both rigid and convinced we already knew every damn thing there was to know. When in truth, any bum on the street could have showed us shit we couldn't see standing right in each other's faces. We did a lot of talking, but very little listening. We were too busy trying to prove our own point to realize the other could have been making a relevant one. The problem wasn't that we didn't love one another; we were just too set in our ways. Stubbornness is a sucker punch that can knock out any couple in the first round.

Our spiritual leader, Pastor Gregory Pollard, has helped us work through a lot of our disputes. He is in our age group and has been married to the same woman for eighteen years. As a pastor, he most definitely knows about conflict resolution. He brings a spiritual element to helping us resolve disputes that a therapist probably couldn't. I don't want anybody telling me anything about myself who doesn't know me. Pastor Pollard knows us and has been in our lives for the last six years.

He is always fair to both sides, and he reaches us in a way that neither feels judged. His swagger and fatherly wisdom make it easy for us to talk about what's really going on in our home. It's comforting to have a man of God say to us, "Okay, here is the biblical way to work through what's happening in your marriage, but you have to do the work to fix it."

My mind is always on how we can repair the tears in our love. If we could do it all over again, I would make sure we did the 12-step counseling thing before saying, "I do." God knows, it would probably be more for me, than us. I wasn't very upfront with Cynthia in the beginning. I took it upon myself to cover up and fix things. I left her in the dark more times than I can count. I didn't handle things fairly; the right thing would have been to put it all on the table and let it do what it do.

I had more of a Captain Save 'Em mentality, when I should have been sitting my wife down and telling her, *"Look, baby, here's the situation…I'm not quite sure how I'm going to fix it, but I just want you to be in the loop and maybe we can figure the shit out together."* It's not an excuse, but part of me knew it didn't take much to put Cynthia in a panic. I thought keeping her in the dark would help me avoid the pressure of her feeling stressed, but all it really ever did was made a bad situation worse.

Cynthia's Standby

I'm only a celebrity in the eyes of our viewers. On the inside, I'm just Cynthia – Peter's wife, Noelle's mom. Unfortunately, people are mainly interested in what's on the outside. They're excited to meet and have a Canon moment with the *Housewives'* Cynthia. They want to hear the complete rundown on how I just got off the phone with NeNe, Peter's in Jamaica doing his coffee gig and Noelle is preparing for her first year in high school. It's amusing that the exchanges and questions are pretty similar to what I would get if I bumped into an old friend I grew up with. It's an interesting and surreal dynamic.

With a faithful allegiance, viewers connect to us on so many levels. If I say blue eye shadow is hideous, women will get up in arms and stop wearing it. It only took one or two incidents for me to learn I needed to always be aware of the power of my words. Like the time I was cast for a swimsuit show during Miami Fashion Week. I was filming the day I received the call telling me I had been booked.

After hanging up the phone, I turned to Malorie and jokingly said, "Well, I gotta get this body swimsuit-ready. Guess I'll go throw up my breakfast." Every bulimic support organization in North America sent me letters, emails and tweets about the comment. The outrage blindsided me. People didn't always seem to get my humor. They took things as literal statements that I merely intended as fun. It made me cognizant of making even innocent jokes. I would get so tickled filtering through all the groups I had to be careful not to offend: PETA, vegetarians, tree huggers, asphalt kissers, cornflake lovers and God knows who else. *Geez!*

I am dissected in every possible measure – from the words that leave my mouth, to my outfit choices and especially my hairstyles. One season, I received a letter about my side ponytail being "too messy." There is also what I call the virtual producer criticisms, where fans tell me who I should be sharing scenes with. They give me feedback like, I'm not hanging with NeNe enough, or I'm hanging with her too much. Worst of all, are the creepy requests for romantic bedroom action between Peter and me. It's an impossible task to satisfy every fan who watches the show, so I don't even try.

I can honestly say I had fun shooting Season 5. I put myself out there and owned everything I said and did. I was past the disappointment of feeling hated and misunderstood. In my former career, people liked me simply because I was a decent person. My television job was the contrary, with people hating or loving me based on a three-minute scene. I never saw how three minutes could possibly give people enough insight to feel either away.

What I now know for sure is that I'm stronger than I ever thought possible. I have never believed in coincidences, and I know fate had everything to do with the path I chose. I was supposed to move to Atlanta, marry Peter Thomas, lose all my money and be on television. It was all part of God's divine plan for me. I know what I can do, but only He knows how much I can take. When I thought I would break, he took root in me and pushed me past my biggest obstacles, but he never took me out of a situation. It's like he was saying, *"You're going to stay right there in the darkness, Cynthia, until you find your way to complete wholeness and happiness."*

I have grown to be fearless in that I am not afraid to lose. Most people are settled into who they are or who they think they are. I am not strapped to any perception of preconceived notion about the direction I should be going. I could wake up tomorrow, quit the show and move to India. I am determined to follow my spirit, whether it makes sense to the masses or not. I just do me, and what my heart drives me to do. My new life's mission is to figure out who I am and resist the temptation of boxing myself in. Every day I'm discovering new strands of life within me, and each sunrise is another chance for me to press toward the mark of a higher calling.

Peter's Standby

Cynthia once told me that a close friend of mine said she may not get the better end of the deal if she got involved with me. Cynthia didn't tell me about the conversation until months after it happened. It hurt me that she waited so long to share it. I never confronted the asshole who made the comment, but I held on to the hateration and used it as a weapon to fight off my critics.

I was stupid in thinking our marriage would be a pact between just the two of us and our kids. I didn't know a lot of other side deals were laced with Cynthia becoming my other half. She has strong relationships with influential friends, and she allows their opinions to offset hers. Life in Atlanta with me meant no more summers in Martha's Vineyard or weekends in the Hamptons. I represented only a simple life with a mediocre restaurateur (whose time had probably already come and gone).

Her people saw me in a light that I had never viewed myself. I thought I had beaten the odds when I left the streets of Brooklyn to better my life. I thought I was making a difference when I created a music conference to show kids how they could be down with the industry. I thought I had made a new lane for myself when I went to L.A. (having never worked in television) and executive produced a syndicated awards show. I thought my name spoke for itself when I went to London and took over Rush Management, but my achievements still didn't cut it in her circles. I had stuff to prove to people I didn't even know. I had never dealt with anything like it, because my friends didn't have the power to sway my decisions.

Marriage is a union that is for the betterment of the couple and the next generation they create. Even going into holy matrimony madly in love with Cynthia, I knew I wouldn't wake up every morning liking her. I didn't take an oath to like her every second of the day. That's a childish mindset. My commitment before God and our families was to love her solemnly, through thick and thin; 'til death do us part. She knows as long as she wants it, I will always do everything in my power to make us work.

Beyoncé's "Love on Top" song is one of my favorite lyrical flows of all time; the words resonate. She has one hell of a grip on what real love looks like. Even at her young age, she already has it down to a science. The song made me fall in love with her! If I am ever in the same room with Beyoncé for even five minutes, Jay gon have some serious problems with me.

One day I was driving and the song came on the radio. The words hit me in my chest so strong that I stopped and texted Cynthia, "You need to put my love on top." She texted me back, "I will." I read her response and replied, "You're whacked!" What the hell? I tell my woman to put my damn love on top and she sends me back a dry ass "I will." I set it up for her, but she fell right through the cracks. She didn't get it!

The purest thing on the planet is sweet, true love. When a couple loves like the words Beyoncé wrote, they will go through hell and back to preserve it. Sometimes, I just need to hear Cynthia say, *"Peter Thomas will never turn his back on me, and nobody in this world can hold me down like he does."*

Cynthia was at a major turning point in her life when she decided to move to Georgia. Twenty years of gracing magazine covers and being the face of countless brands hadn't made her the star I knew she could be. I didn't know how big she could become, I just knew the situation would be better. If nothing else, she would be closer to her mom, living in cleaner air and free from a $5,000 monthly lease on an 800-square-foot apartment.

She took the risk and it made me love her even more. A woman is supposed to feel safe with her man, and a man is supposed to provide for his woman. Losing Uptown was a blessing and I didn't even realize it. I thank God that at the age of forty-nine, I didn't have a pot to piss in or a window to throw it out. I am grateful for all the painful lessons that made me a better, stronger, wiser man. If not for them, I would never have known the DNA and true character of the person I live with, and she wouldn't know mine.

I wouldn't change anything about how Cynthia and I came to be. If there had been a different set of circumstances, we probably would not have ended up with the same results. I love my wife, my life, my kids and

Noelle (*my special number six*). What it boils down to is that everything in life can be defined in the context of mathematics. Life is no different than a math problem. If you change one single variable, the outcome will be totally different. Knowing that, I live a life free of regrets.

I can't change anything that happened yesterday, all I can do is make improvements on the day that follows. One of life's most beautiful qualities is that we are all given the same number of hours in a day to make a difference. Money, good looks or fame can't add a second of credit to anyone's pot. From Bill Gates to Peter Thomas, we all have only twenty-four hours in a day to make it happen. Yeah, Bill is sitting on about seventy billion more bills than me, but even if he wrote a check for every penny he has in the bank, it still wouldn't buy him a minute more in his day than I have in mine.

Cynthia's Please Remain Seated

Before Noelle was born, I would pick a country and go there to soul search for a month, without a lover or travel companion. I used it as an annual thirty-day excursion to clear my head. I want Noelle to have the freedom and privilege to live that same life. If she takes nothing else from me, I pray that she possesses my spirit of adventure and inquisitiveness about the world.

She's very strong and will be a more phenomenal woman than I could ever be. At her age, I didn't have her sense of awareness or the advanced thought processes she has. It wasn't ingrained in me that I could be, or do, anything I wanted. I didn't have that rite of passage until adulthood. At thirteen, when most kids are just starting to gain their independence, Noelle already knows exactly what she wants to do in life. She is focused on being an actress and singer. She would rather do nothing, than something she isn't passionate about.

She got it honest, because her father is the same way. His hunger to be an actor flows like blood through his veins. Leon has always had a bold confidence about him. Back when we dated, it would blow me away. I asked him on many occasions how he came to be that way. I wanted to know what had led him to believe he was so great. He told me he had been raised to believe such. No one ever challenged whether he could or would become an actor. It was treated as something that was inevitable.

Leon and I used that same blueprint to raise Noelle. Consequently, if something does not hinge on the core of who she is, she becomes disinterested. It is a kind of greatness that she doesn't even realize is great. It's such a fundamental strength to have in a child that it has even taught me not to apologize for how I am or change who I am. As aggravating and annoying as it is to raise such an unyielding child, I respect the hell out of her. If I had a third of her gumption at the same age, I would have been out of this world awesome.

It seems like I've lived at the fork in the road my whole existence. I have never been content in any set place, because my instinct always told me there was more or something else I should be doing. Some people are alive but they aren't living. I don't want to look back on my life and feel like I lived stuck in a box. I want to be free, happy, at peace and in love. I want to look back at the fourth quarter of my life and say, "I did that."

I know without any question that Peter Thomas loves me, and he knows I completely love him. We have a commonality and a spiritual connection that speaks without using words. If our journey ends, it won't be over infidelity. It'll be because we both decided that we've gone as far as we were supposed to go together. Our marriage is about loving each other enough to be fully committed, but also letting go if it doesn't work anymore. We live our lives day to day. It's hard to predict what's next for us. I've never been one to try and forecast what will happen next month or next year. All I know is that we are supposed to be making this voyage together.

Peter and I still disagree on a lot of things and we don't wake up every morning singing, "Oh Happy Day." Since we are still very much individuals, we do not always go about things in a harmonious fashion. I've gotten to know every part of him. I have seen his loveable and not so nice places. I've seen him up in his balcony and down in the basement. I know him wholly and what I'm working with. Understanding his heart allows me to genuinely love him for who he is.

When our run on the show is done, I want to take some time off and intensely focus on us. The utopia afterlife would be Peter and I settling into marital happiness, me being able to enjoy the remainder of Noelle's teenage years and continuing to change lives through my work at The Bailey Agency. I can't wait to have unscheduled, unstructured Cynthia time to discover where my destiny will take me.

The Real Housewives of Atlanta is an opportunity of a lifetime! I only have to show up and be me – the script is whatever's going on in my life. Not everyone gets to wake up and play themselves on national television. Opening myself up allowed for so much to happen that would have never occurred, had I not placed my life under a microscope. I want to leave the series having changed my life in every way – spiritually, physically and financially.

As raw as my growth process has been, I am grateful that I was able to uncover who I really am and what I'm made of. I don't have to wonder about what would have happened had I not moved from New York to Atlanta or married the man of my dreams – I already know. I don't want to just live my life; I want to understand it. I hope to never stop hitting those crossroads in my life. It's what has kept me going.

Whatever my claim to fame will be still hasn't happened. My intuition tells me that when people recall the life of Cynthia Bailey, I won't be remembered for my occupation as a model or an Atlanta Housewife. I think my biggest moment and thickest chapter will be my next one. I'm no longer afraid of the unknown; I receive it. Every time I make a choice, I know it only leads me closer to where I'm going.

My story is still being written.

Peter's Please Remain Seated

The Real Housewives of Atlanta made Cynthia and me somewhat of an "it" black couple. Cynthia was revealed as a down woman who had her man's back, even in the face of extreme opposition. People saw me standing tall through our trials but they also witnessed my wrath. Once I released all the anger that had been suffocating me, people began to see me as a relatable, ordinary guy.

In the past year, I've been approached by hundreds of black men who commend me on how I have conducted myself in recent seasons. They see me as strong and positive – not extra. It feels good to be appreciated and understood. Hearing the generous words of encouragement from so many black males makes me careful about every scene I step into. I'm now more aware of how my actions might create an effect I don't want.

God put Cynthia and me on the same track to come together and shine in a way that we couldn't without the other. I want us to fight to stay centered and in love. As recently as May of 2013, I called Pastor Pollard for marital support. Cynthia and I had a big blow up, and I was having one of the hardest weeks of our marriage. I didn't know if we would make it through it. I don't mind yelling and screaming to reach a better place, but it's a problem when a disagreement leaves my wife viewing me differently from how I really am.

It messed with my head bad, and I had a mini-breakdown. I didn't know how to fix what had happened or how to file away all the painful shit that had been said. We needed an old-school, third-party intervention. I wanted us to get out the hostility that had been breeding inside of us. We couldn't move beyond the issue until we could figure out a way to agree, or agree to disagree. Our schedules kept getting in the way of us sitting down with Pastor Pollard, but by God's grace, we managed to work through it without him.

With all we have faced, I'm happy and surprised that my wife and I are still together. The *Housewives* franchise has had a lot of marital casualties – *a total of eighteen to be exact.* The reality scene is not for everyone. It will truly test a marriage to see what it can endure. I credit our spirituality and faith for holding us down. Every couple should sit down with a counselor or spiritual advisor at least twice a year, if for no other reason than to check in with each other.

Men cannot be afraid to stand up and be the spiritual giants in their households. A man should get up and go to church on Sundays, even if his woman doesn't. Her lack of participation shouldn't keep him from worshipping. If she sees him making moves, she'll eventually follow. A woman is naturally inquisitive, and anytime her man goes somewhere without her, she is most definitely going to ask where he's been and what he did. A brutha sharing his experience after visiting the house of the Lord, will put his mate in such awe, she'll be hanging on to his every word.

I have not said it to him, but Pastor Pollard has been a light that has helped me to see down plenty of dark, dismal roads. He is a man of great spiritual wisdom and every word he has ever shared with me fed my spirit. I deeply appreciate him and his involvement in my relationship with Cynthia. Yielding to a higher power has definitely strengthened my base with her.

I'm careful not to take Cynthia or any aspect of our lives for granted. We continue to build on our faith, our love and our businesses. We're fortunate that bar ONE has become a national tourist attraction (*where grown black women come looking for Peter Thomas*). Cynthia is inspiring so many young girls to believe they can come out of a little, country place like Alabama and pursue their dreams. We both get off on the idea of using our aspirations to empower people.

Nothing is promised, so we work hard at maintaining humility and gratefulness, which keeps us grounded. I wake up every morning and ask her, "Honey, what are we going to do next?" Life has us on a crazy track where sometimes she's going east and I'm going west, but our travels are always for the benefit of our family. We exist for only a moment in time, but no matter how much carry-on baggage life throws at us, I pray we'll always manage to catch our flight and take the trip…*together*!

Cynthia Bailey-Thomas

Supermodel. Supermom. Super (house)wife.

C YNTHIA BAILEY IS one of the stars of the hit, BRAVO reality show, *The Real Housewives of Atlanta*. The Alabama-born beauty moved to New York City twenty-five years ago to pursue a career as a fashion model. With nothing more than a high school homecoming queen crown and a few local beauty pageants under her belt, the Wilhelmina Models agency signed her to a five-year contract. Her first booking, an *Essence* magazine cover, was one of the highest-selling issues in the magazine's history.

Shortly after signing with Wilhelmina, Cynthia relocated to Paris and Milan, where she became a familiar face, strutting down the runways of Fashion Week. After living abroad, she returned to New York where she was hand-selected for both a Maybelline and an Oil of Olay campaign. Magazine editorials for *Vogue*, *Elle*, *Glamour*, and *Vanity Fair* quickly followed. Over the years, Cynthia has been the brand face for Macy's, Neiman Marcus, Lord & Taylor, Saks Fifth Avenue, Talbots, Chico's and Bergdorf Goodman.

Cynthia touts the birth of her daughter, Noelle Forde Robinson, as her greatest accomplishment. She credits her strong will and solid spiritual background for her success in life and business. She is the CEO of The Bailey Agency School of Fashion in Atlanta, Georgia, where she lives with her restaurateur husband, Peter Thomas.

Peter Thomas
The man. The myth. The mogul.

A NEW YORK NATIVE, Peter Thomas is the founder and CEO of The Peter Thomas Entertainment Group (PTEG). He has been long recognized as a pioneer in creating and producing sophisticated nightlife, dining and lifestyle enterprises. With a career in the entertainment industry spanning more than 30 years, Peter is known for delivering unparalleled experiences in nightclubs, restaurants, entertainment and award show production.

Peter embodies the spirit of a true entrepreneur and has laid the foundation for a successful brand of bar ONE lounges. The flagship operation opened in Atlanta's historic Grant Park area in October of 2011. The runaway success of bar ONE, Atlanta set the stage for national brand recognition, and the franchise is now expanding to Charlotte, North Carolina. Thomas hopes to bring its unique and unforgettable dining experience to customers throughout major U. S. markets.

This restaurateur, business mogul and father of five resides in Atlanta, Georgia, with his wife, Cynthia Bailey-Thomas.